Theory and Practi

Constructi

With a Detailed, Practical Method for Tuning

William Braid White

Alpha Editions

This edition published in 2023

ISBN : 9789357946094

Design and Setting By
Alpha Editions
www.alphaedis.com
Email - info@alphaedis.com

As per information held with us this book is in Public Domain.
This book is a reproduction of an important historical work. Alpha Editions uses the best technology to reproduce historical work in the same manner it was first published to preserve its original nature. Any marks or number seen are left intentionally to preserve its true form.

SOME REMARKS BY THE PUBLISHER.

For many years we have been receiving at the office of The Music Trade Review constant inquiries for sources from which information might be gleaned regarding the theory and practice of tone production as applied to the piano. It has therefore been obvious to all who have given this subject the slightest consideration that there has been a lack of book information which should be at the hand of the student and the seeker of knowledge regarding scale draughting and other essentials relating to piano construction. Some years ago, after careful consideration of this subject, special topics along these lines were assigned to the author of this work, who was well fitted for the task before him, and as a result of more than two years of conscientious study and research, the "Theory and Practice of Pianoforte Building" is put forth as representing in a concrete form a work of technical knowledge which hitherto has been unobtainable to the student.

The necessity of acquiring some knowledge of the principles of mechanics before proceeding to the study of scale design is admitted. Such knowledge, together with that of the principles of the acoustics as they apply to musical sounds produced by vibrating strings, is essential to a correct understanding of the fundamental ideas underlying true pianoforte design.

To know a piano accurately one must understand the laws governing tone quality, and how the propagation and transmission of sound is produced as well as the pitch and intensity of sound. And there are thousands of men to-day in the various factories who are anxious to obtain sources of information from which to gain a more correct knowledge of a profession which should take high rank among industrial pursuits.

Owing to the gradual changes which have been wrought in all industries through the abandonment of the apprentice system, there is more need for instruction books than ever before.

A factory operative, according to the present plan, may know thoroughly but one department of the business, but he can become more useful to himself and his employers when he possesses a knowledge of all branches. In the piano trade particularly there must be a correct knowledge of piano building, else there can be no advance, and with our old piano makers rapidly passing away there is need for a healthy school of new inventors, so that wherever possible, improvements may be made and defects remedied. These can only be accomplished by the possession of a knowledge of all the intricate principles involved in piano making.

We feel that in presenting a work of this kind we are offering a volume which will meet with the approval of those who seek knowledge, for while there are great trade and technical schools which are the fountains of inspiration for various trades, the science of piano making is not included as a branch in any of them. It is therefore evident that knowledge must be gained outside, for piano schools there are none. To every mind seeking information there should be knowledge given, and we believe that a work of this kind must be of value to an industry wherein there is such a dearth of reliable text books.

It will be seen by examination that all of the practical problems which are to be considered by the scale draughtsmen have been fairly treated in this volume and yet the desire of the author has been throughout to avoid tiresome details. Condensation is one of the recognized laws of our day, and in producing this technical work the author has labored to create a volume of convenient size which shall be of service to the student, and to the advanced thinker as well, on account of the accuracy with which the subjects are treated.

This book is not in the remotest sense a history of piano building or development, and it should not be so considered; in fact it has been deemed wise to dip into historical matters only to the extent of showing the application of an enduring principle rather than to give credit to a number of deserving inventors who have worked along special lines. A treatment of worthy inventions would require a much larger volume than this; and while there are many inventors who have given to the world special devices of value, it has not been considered timely to describe them in this volume or to enter into an exposé of their merits or demerits. We may say that this is not a critical work but rather one which we trust may be eminently practical in its mission as an instructive and an educational force.

We may add in closing that the "Theory and Practice of Pianoforte Building" is the only work of its kind ever put forth in the English language, and we have every confidence that it will find a growing demand among music trade people everywhere.

EDWARD LYMAN BILL.

Editorial Rooms,
The Music Trade Review,

NEW YORK, May, 1906.

CHAPTER I.
INTRODUCTORY REMARKS.

The development of the modern American pianoforte presents a most interesting study to the practical member of the musical industries as well as to the pianist. For it is possible to view the subject with equal facility from the standpoints of both. Descended through a clearly defined line of ancestry from the ancient psaltery, and showing traces of the various steps in its evolution throughout its entire modern form, the pianoforte of to-day is essentially the product of all the ages. There have not been wanting a sufficient number of writers upon the history and ancestry of the instrument; but an exposition of the correct principles of design has not hitherto appeared in the English language, at least in a form that possesses permanent value to the American manufacturer. The once classic work of Rimbault is obsolete to-day, even in Europe; while, on the other hand, the various German treatises have been difficult to obtain and necessarily limited in their appeal to an English speaking people, nor have any satisfactory translations of any of them yet been put forth.

Furthermore, the evolution of pianoforte building in this country has proceeded along characteristically American lines and has resulted in the existence to-day of a peculiarly national, advanced and complex type. American pianofortes are universally acknowledged to stand among the highest developments of applied musical craftsmanship, and artists of every degree have willingly given their assent to every claim that has been made for the instruments.

While, however, these facts are easily demonstrable, it would be by no means correct to suppose that the development of the American types of pianoforte has been materially assisted by even a respectable minority of those who have been engaged in constructing them. On the contrary, the magnificent examples of the musical instrument maker's art that grace the homes of musicians and people of culture throughout the United States owe their present high excellence to the labors and skill of a small band of enthusiastic and clever workers. The names of William Hawkins, Jonas Chickering, and Henry Engelhard Steinway should be written in letters of gold above the doors of all institutions devoted to the creation of artistic pianofortes. For it is to the earnest labor and untiring enthusiasm of these men and a few others, working alone and unassisted, that the modern American instrument owes its present proud position.

And this state of affairs has continued to exist until the present day. There are, as there have always been, a few talented and skilful men who have never been content to rest upon their laurels or to desist from continual labor along the lines of musical and mechanical betterment; but such as they stand, and have always stood, alone. The great majority have been glad to accept the improvements of their preceding or contemporaneous masters after the commercial value of the innovations has been demonstrated; but they have always lacked the audacity or capability to strike out into new fields and untrodden pathways.

We may, however, discern a sufficient reason for this timidity on the part of pianoforte makers. The principles that underly the design of the instrument are primarily acoustical. They have never been very easily digested, either by the mechanic or by the man of affairs. And since a knowledge of acoustics has been profoundly developed only within the last sixty years or so, it follows that its application to the design of musical instruments has naturally lagged behind the progress of the science itself. Pianoforte makers are not usually professing scientists or practical musicians; and they have discerned little profit in attempting to keep up with the trend of modern acoustical research, even so far as this has directly affected the principles of musical instrument construction.

The development of the pianoforte has, in fact, proceeded empirically, and has been prosecuted inductively rather than from any *a priori* notions. And while we cannot withhold our admiration from the splendid success that has attended so much of this empirical research, we cannot be blind to the fact that very many modern pianofortes exhibit clearly the inherent defects of such methods. The practical musical mechanician, if he possess the requisite knowledge, is often able to remedy existing faults in tone quality and tone-production. And while studying ways and means for doing this, he cannot but observe innumerable cases of neglected opportunities, or even of positive mistakes. The pure empirical method must always produce a large number of failures. Yet the application of even the elementary principles of Applied Acoustics would frequently prevent the commission of serious sins in design. It is not necessary, of course, that every scale draughtsman or designer should have the results of modern acoustical discovery at his fingers' ends; but it is here insisted that such knowledge, in so far as it relates to musical instruments, is essential to the correct construction of pianofortes.

Tone-production, otherwise than by the human voice, implies both scientific and mechanical problems. Especially is this true of the pianoforte, which, with the exception of the pipe organ, may properly be considered the most complex of artificial devices for the performance of music.

Recognition of this truth and a general improvement in the knowledge of the acoustical and musical principles involved cannot fail to exercise a most beneficial influence upon the future of the American pianoforte.

As has already been remarked, there is a dearth of convenient treatises in the English language that can be said to possess a present value to the earnest student of pianoforte design. The present book is an attempt in the direction of supplying the deficiency. The author has aimed at presenting the various problems pertaining to the art of pianoforte construction with due regard both to their acoustical and mechanical features. No attempt has been made to delve profoundly into the mysteries of sound; but the elementary and basic principles of tone-production have been stated, and their true application to the various stages of pianoforte construction explained. Each step in the making of a pianoforte from beginning to completion has been subjected to analysis, and the correct principles pointed out.

The author believes that the book may be read and comprehended, even by one to whom the very term acoustics has hitherto been unfamiliar. While he does not expect that a study of this book can make the novice a full-fledged scale draughtsman, as it were, overnight, he does expect, on the other hand, to assist those who have already investigated, or who intend to investigate the whole problem, to a clearer and broader comprehension of a beautiful art. If this hope be gratified, much will have been achieved, and no one who has at heart the future of musical industry in America can fail to be encouraged, if nothing else, by the appearance of this condensed work.

The general outline of the book can be explained with little detail. Recognizing, as has already been suggested, the dependence of all right pianoforte making upon the observance of the established principles of acoustics, the author has thought it well, after a short historical sketch of the pianoforte, to make a general statement of the laws that govern the propagation and transmission of sound. It is but a step from this to a concise explanation of the peculiarities of stretched strings and their behavior under varying conditions of excitation, and differing phases of tension, etc. This leads us directly to the discussion of pianoforte strings, their dimensions, and the manner in which they become the agents of sound-production in the instrument.

Continuing our investigations, we pass to the subject of resonance and come naturally to a discussion of the resonating apparatus of the pianoforte.

The framing that holds together these two vital elements is next subjected to analysis and explanation, and finally the mechanisms of percussion and touch are brought under our inquiry and their peculiarities noted and expounded. The remarks upon the draughting of pianoforte scales, that conclude the volume, are necessarily broad and general, since it is quite impossible to indicate with exactitude the actual method to be employed in making mechanical drawings, at least within the limits that the relative importance of the subject imposes on us. Attention has been drawn more particularly to the calculations for shrinkage that are rendered necessary by the vagaries of cast iron, such as is used in the manufacture of metal frames, and to the details of hammer-stroke points and string dimensions, the principles of which have been explained in their proper places within the body of the work.

CHAPTER II.
THE EVOLUTION OF THE PIANOFORTE.

While the present work is by no means intended to serve as an elaborate analysis of pianoforte development, it seems that a proper comprehension of the various principles that are laid down in the course of our argument will be facilitated by a short survey of the evolution of the instrument, undertaken from an historical viewpoint. As we recognize in the pianoforte of to-day the culmination of the musical-mechanical effort of ages, and as a complete study of the results that have been achieved can best be introduced by a preliminary knowledge of the manner in which the various steps towards latter-day excellence have been attained, it seems that we cannot do better than make an attempt to survey the field of pianoforte evolution in a manner broad and general, though necessarily brief.

As was incidentally remarked in the last chapter, we may properly consider the modern pianoforte as essentially the product of all the ages. The origin of stringed instruments is lost in the mists of antiquity, but Greek mythology has supplied us with a most pleasing legend to account for the invention of that pioneer of all stretched-string instruments, the classic lyre. We are told that Hermes, walking one day along the shore, found lying at his feet the shell of a dead tortoise. The intestines of the animal had been dried in the sun and were stretched along the rim of the shell so that when Hermes' foot struck against one of them, a musical sound was given forth and Lo! the lyre was born. Earlier still are the accounts, in the shape of cuneiform or other inscriptions, that show a form of lyre to have been in use among the Assyrians. The biblical descriptions of various stringed instruments, such as the psaltery, or the harp of David, are generally familiar.

While doubtless we need not consider it illogical to trace the beginning of modern stringed instruments, whether they be of the key-board variety or otherwise, to such misty and vague traditions, we must look to more modern times for a true understanding of the causes that operated to produce the key-board. This, the distinguishing feature of the pianoforte family, first arose through the need for a facile means of accompanying the voice in the then newly beginning art of music which required the simultaneous sounding of different tones. Instruments of the organ type were earlier in the field, for we have accounts of the water-organ in the writings of the historians of the later Roman Empire. The earliest form of key-board seems to have been introduced in Europe in the latter part of the eleventh century A. D. At about the same period we hear of a stringed instrument called the organistrum, having three strings, one of which was in connection with a number of tangents which were adapted to be pushed in upon it so as to sound different segments and produce different notes. Later we find that the ecclesiastical musicians were in the habit of using more or less complicated monochords for the purpose of training their pupils in the plain-chants of the church. These monochords gradually became more complex and finally were mounted on a kind of sound board in groups and thus became no longer monochords but trichords, tetrachords, or polychords. The next step was obviously to furnish the instrument with a set of balanced key-levers borrowed from the organ and with tangents to connect the keys with the strings, these latter coming from the organistrum. Thus we have at once the famous clavichord.

But this was not the only form of keyed instrument that was thus early devised. We learn that the psaltery had contemporaneously been fitted with keys. There were two forms of this famous instrument, one trapezoid and one triangular. When both of these had been fitted with keys there were two more distinct forms of keyed instruments; differences which had a large influence upon the later development of the type.

These three instruments were thus developed into the accepted forms that were in general use during the seventeenth century and later; becoming respectively the clavichord, harpsichord and spinet. It is from these that the pianoforte is directly sprung. The harpsichord, as its name implies, resembled a harp laid on its back and enclosed in a case, while the strings were plucked, by quills set on jacks, mounted on the keys. The natural shape of the harpsichord, therefore, was similar to that of the modern grand pianoforte and it derived this form from its direct relationship to the early keyed forms of the triangular psaltery. The harpsichord had been a favorite for a long time when Bartolomeo Cristofori, a maker of Florence, completed in 1709 the invention of a hammer action to replace the quilled jack at the end of the harpsichord key. Thus was made possible the production of dynamic effects, of which the harpsichord action had never been capable except through the employment of various mechanical devices, such as swells and double or triple banks of keys with jacks and quills to match. The hammer-action of Cristofori as completed by him in 1726 shows a remarkable similarity to the mechanisms that are still to be found in certain forms of square pianofortes. He succeeded in producing an acceptable form of escapement and a damping device as well, although as the date shows, not until after several years of experimenting and improving upon the original design. Examination shows that Cristofori's action differs in no essential respect from the square pianoforte actions that we have mentioned. There is the upper and under hammer, the jack working on a groove in the key, the escapement device to determine the travel of the jack, the back-check, and the damper. Every feature that is essential to provide escapement, repetition and damping is found here. Cristofori was, however, obliged to make many changes in the construction of his "gravicembalo col piano e forte" to provide the increased stiffness necessitated by the different manner of exciting the strings. His work, curiously enough, was not taken up after his death by any other Italian harpsichord maker, and it remained for a German to continue his experiments and bring them to a practical and commercial success. Only two pianofortes by Cristofori are known to exist, and one of these is in the Metropolitan Museum of Art, New York.

Gottfried Silbermann, who took up the work of Cristofori, built several grand pianofortes towards the end of the first half of the eighteenth century, and there still exist at Potsdam some of these that were sold by him to Frederick the Great. These instruments appear to be essentially founded upon the work of Cristofori, and the superior workmanship and better adjustment of them do not serve to disguise the evident fact that Silbermann, while improving in details, did not discover any new principles either in action or otherwise.

Somewhat later we hear of Zumpe, who was apparently struck with the idea of adapting the pianoforte hammer to the square-shaped clavichord, which was not deep enough to take the Silbermann action, thus producing a veritable square pianoforte. Zumpe's device contained no provision for escapement, which fault was afterwards corrected by the celebrated inventor Stein. Mozart speaks of the merits of Stein and joyfully describes how his mechanism prevented the blocking of the hammers. Mozart used one of Stein's pianofortes during the rest of his life.

The name of Stein is justly famous among the early pianoforte makers. He was responsible, with the able assistance of his daughter Nanette, for the Viennese type of pianoforte, which was for long such a favorite over the heavier and more solid English style on account of its surprising delicacy and lightness of touch. After her marriage, Nanette Stein, in partnership with her husband Streicher, made many other improvements, and her pianofortes were used by Beethoven and others. The firm of Streicher still existed in Vienna a few years ago.

At this point, namely at the beginning of the nineteenth century, we begin to hear of three revolutionary figures; a Frenchman, an Englishman and an American. These are Erard, Broadwood and Hawkins.

Pierre Sebastian Erard settled in Paris during the latter part of the eighteenth century as a maker of harps and harpsichords. Shortly before the breaking out of the French revolution, Erard came to London and began to make harps and pianofortes. In the meantime he was continually working to improve his instruments and was responsible for many useful inventions, such as the up-bearing to the strings by means of the "agraffe." His chief claim to the consideration of pianoforte makers is due, however, to his invention of the "double repetition" action which was perfected by him in

1821, after many years of unsuccessful experiment. This action, with slight modification, is used at the present day in all grand pianofortes, and its manifold excellences have never been yet surpassed. Erard took out a large number of patents, which were put into use by his successors, and the house founded by him is still in existence and one of the most famous in France or indeed in the world.

John Broadwood, the great English inventor and manufacturer, who also has his name perpetuated in the continued and flourishing career of the firm that he founded, was originally a workman in the shop of Tschudi or Shudi, a London harpsichord maker. He rose from an apprenticeship to the head of the house of Shudi and finally turned his attention to the improvement of the pianoforte. He had early been the recipient of the knowledge of Backers, the inventor of the so-called English action, and when he came to build pianofortes on his own account, this experience was made to bear practical fruit. Broadwood's first achievement was in the re-designing of the square piano of Zumpe. About the year 1780 he entirely altered its construction, set the tuning pins at the back of the case, and added dampers and pedals. He next set about the improvement of the grand, and divided the bridge, giving a separate bass bridge and permitting the striking point of the hammers on the strings to be adjusted with correctness, something that had never been done before. This completed the divorce of the pianoforte from the harpsichord. With the addition of the action invented by Backers, Broadwood's pianofortes became at once a standard of quality and excellence and until the introduction of iron framing stood alone.

We now come to Hawkins. This remarkable man was an engineer of Philadelphia, English by birth but American by adoption. In the year 1800 he produced an upright pianoforte, the first of its kind. This instrument, though it was not a commercial success, was remarkable for the fact that Hawkins in it anticipated so many of the ideas that have since become essential to modern instruments. He had an independent iron frame supporting the sound-board, a mechanical tuning device, and metal action frames. His action, too, had many features that have since been adopted. Unfortunately, the tone was so poor that the instrument was a failure from the start. His ideas in regard to upright pianoforte construction were not allowed to languish, however, and the labors of Wornum, who followed Southwell, were at last successful in producing, in 1826, a practical action which at once settled the destiny of the upright. This action had as its peculiar feature the "bridle tape," which is now such a necessary element of the upright pianoforte. He also introduced the centre pin and flange.

At this point we begin to come to the great dividing line between the early and the modern pianoforte. The introduction of metal framing marks this division and it is from here that the American instrument begins its independent and extraordinarily successful career. Indeed, the development of American instruments is bound up with the almost concurrent progress of ideas as to metal framing.

Although the first application of metal to pianofortes, not considering the unfortunately abortive invention of Hawkins, may be credited to William Allen, an Englishman, yet we must look to the United States for the pioneer in the modern conception of metal bracing. The man in question, Alpheus Babcock, was a Boston maker and had been originally an apprentice of Crehore, who appears to have made the first American pianoforte. Babcock applied his invention in Boston in the form of a cast metal plate for a square pianoforte about the year 1822 and this date is most memorable in that it marks the epoch of the strictly modern conception of the instrument. Continuing the consideration of this National school of design, we find that the celebrated Jonas Chickering produced, in 1840, a cast-iron plate for grand pianofortes, having the string-plate, agraffe-bridge and resistance-bars cast solid in one piece. This revolutionary invention unquestionably paved the way for the wonderful American productions of later years and at once placed the American pianoforte upon a plane of excellence that has never been altogether reached by its competitors in other parts of the world. European makers were at first slow to appreciate the eminently valuable nature of the invention of Chickering, and until lately the solid cast plate was not extensively used in Europe outside of Germany. The house of Collard and Collard, which had the services of Stewart, the assistant of Chickering for many years, was, however, most progressive in this respect and for long was the only London firm which made grand pianofortes with the iron plate cast in one piece. The celebrated house of Broadwood, after much experimenting, produced a form of iron plate for grands that was somewhat different in principle from that of Chickering. In this type, the body of the structure was cast complete, but instead of the multiplicity of braces, we find only two. One of these runs parallel with the line of the vertically-strung bass strings at the extreme bass end of the instrument, while the other crosses the plate in a diagonal direction from near the middle of the agraffe-bridge to the point of greatest tension. Both of these bars are cast separate from the body of the plate and secured to it by means of bolts and nuts. Such a method has usually been characteristic of European as opposed to American methods, but the Broadwoods, about fifteen years ago, brought out a decided novelty in their "Barless Grand." This remarkable instrument has a plate of cast steel and is entirely without braces or bars of any kind, the necessary stiffness being gained through the tensile strength of the metal employed and the use of a number of turned up flanges along the sides of the structure, these being screwed into the case of the pianoforte at equal intervals on its periphery.

As to the further development of the grand pianoforte, we may look to the progress of the Chickerings and the Steinways in America and to the Broadwoods in England, the Erards in France and the Bechsteins and Blüthners in Germany. These makers are considered here because they have all contributed in no small degree to the development of the instrument as an artistic product and because they have all been responsible for some radical improvement that has later become essential to the make-up of a good pianoforte. We need only mention the Steinway cupola plate, fan-like disposition of strings, overstrung bass, duplex scale and capo d'astro bar to give the reader some idea of the many inventions that have sprung from the fertile brains of the members of this house. The other houses, notably that of Chickering in this country, and Broadwood in England, have been prolific in improvements, and the development of the grand pianoforte has consequently been rapid and successful from the musical and scientific, no less than from the commercial view-point. The history of the type in more recent years is familiar to all, however, and it is unnecessary to enlarge upon it here.

If we have seemed, hitherto, to have neglected proper consideration of the upright and square forms of pianoforte, the fault is more apparent than real. For there are two good reasons why discussion of these types should have been delayed. In the first place, the square is already obsolescent if not obsolete, while on the other hand the development of the upright into a commercially successful and largely produced instrument has only come about in recent years. This sketch would, of course, be incomplete without brief consideration of them and we shall therefore devote some space to this end.

As has already been indicated, the square piano may be considered as having a genesis quite distinct from the grand or upright. It was developed, as we know, by Zumpe, whose purpose was to fit the hammer action to the body of a clavichord. Thus, when we consider the different roots from which the clavichord and spinet-harpsichord types were themselves evolved, and the direct descent of the grand pianoforte from the latter, the entirely separate and distinct growth of the square is easily discerned. This distinction is most interesting at the present day, when the glory of the square has departed and its days are numbered.

The evolution of the square pianoforte in America has been recorded with faithful detail by Spillane in his "History of the American Pianoforte," and the reader will find in that work an abundance of material to satisfy any curiosity that may possess him. Incidentally it may be remarked that the idea of cross-stringing the bass had been applied to clavichords as early as the time of Händel; so that the overstringing of the square pianoforte came about quite naturally, especially after the improvements of John Broadwood the

First. On the other hand, this principle was for long overlooked in the design of the other popular types; so much so, in fact, that European grands and uprights are still to be found in plenty with straight stringing throughout.

The chief reasons for the gradual decline in the popularity of the square may be traced almost as much to social and economic as to artistic and mechanical causes, although these latter had the greater influence in shaping the ultimate destiny of the type. The square was developed in the United States until the native American product left all imitators and rivals far behind, but even at that the fundamental defects of construction could never be overcome entirely. The great gap in the middle of the structure, required for the passage of the hammers, entailed dangerous weakness, against which no reasonable weight of iron bracing has ever seemed to prevail. Again, the fact that the bass keys, where the strength of the blow and the leverage of the action need to be greatest, were the shortest of all, while the extreme treble keys were longest, always tended to destroy the touch proportions and entailed much counter-balancing and other operations which were, however, but makeshifts at the best. Moreover, the development of the grand type led to rivalry among those makers who confined themselves chiefly to the square, with the result that the latter was made more and more heavy and cumbrous in an effort to catch up with the fundamental advantage which the grand pianoforte possessed on account of its superior design. Besides, the square was never a thing of beauty, and its increasing size was by no means an advantage in this respect, so that when the rapidly growing population of the great American cities began to make living room continually more valuable, the claims of the small, powerful, elegant, and moderate-priced upright soon were successfully asserted. As a last consideration, it should be mentioned that the makers of square pianofortes were never able to apply to it a mechanism having the elasticity and rapid repetition that belong to the Erard grand action or the tape-check device of Wornum, which is universal in the upright.

In view of all these disadvantages, it is no longer a matter for wonderment that the upright pianoforte succeeded the square as a bidder for domestic favor, while the larger and more highly evolved grand remained the choice of professional musicians.

The commercial development of the upright pianoforte, as we have remarked, began at a comparatively recent period. In this country, owing to the popularity of the square, we find that the upright was late in coming into favor. Its development, however, had been going on in Europe since the beginning of the nineteenth century. The "cabinet" piano of Southwell and the "upright grand" of Hawkins were examples of early attempts in this line, but it remained for the genius of Robert Wornum to place the upright instrument on a truly practical footing. This was accomplished through his invention of "the tape-check action," which at once put the upright pianoforte upon an equal plane of efficiency with the prevailing types and assured its rapid adoption. By the end of the first half of the nineteenth century the upright piano had become firmly established as the home instrument throughout Europe, and about the same time began to appear among American products. As soon as American manufacturers took hold of it, they set about making vast improvements upon European models; and we may properly date the modern development of the upright from this time. Americans were responsible for the adoption of overstrung iron-framed scales, and for the increase in size and power which now makes our best instruments of this class equal, if not superior, to the grands of a few years ago.

The later history of the upright, not less than of the grand, is a simple record of continuous improvement in details of workmanship and material, in beauty of case design and in scientific construction of scale. It is not necessary, for the purpose of this short sketch, to enter into the familiar modern history of manufacturing the various types of pianoforte, either in this country or abroad; but we may note, incidentally, that European makers have adopted more and more American inventions and improvements, so that the modern, up-to-date pianoforte owes a great part of its present efficiency to the genius of the great American makers, although these, of course, have worked along the great principles that Broadwood, Chickering, Steinway, Weber, Knabe, Erard and others laid down.

Thus we have surveyed, though truly in a somewhat hurried manner, the interesting history of the growth and development of the pianoforte of to-day. The reader will forgive the brief and sketchy nature of this bird's-eye view, when he recollects that our purpose in this book is to lay down the correct principles of modern design, rather than to analyze those principles from an historical standpoint. Some of the laws that we shall have occasion to expound have already been noted here. In the succeeding chapters these and others will be considered in the light of their scientific and practical application.

CHAPTER III.
DESCRIPTION OF THE MODERN PIANOFORTE.

The pianoforte of to-day is the most complex and ingenious of musical instruments. With the possible exception of the pipe-organ, there is no existing tone apparatus that combines within itself the product of so many varied industries. Both as to the raw material and the finished parts, this instrument draws its tonal charm, in the ultimate analysis, as much from the saw-mill, the machine shop and the iron foundry as from the forest and the mine. Trees of the forest, ore from the mines—even the wooly coats of the peaceful sheep—alike contribute their share to the completion of the wonderful product of musico-mechanical ingenuity that we recognize in the modern pianoforte.

In such circumstances as these, it is easy to understand that the commercial production of these instruments is a formidable undertaking. To the musical and technical skill that is essential must now be added large capital and a great manufacturing plant. The moderate prices at which it is at present possible to sell pianofortes would not be maintained for a moment without this modern system of productive concentration and distributive expansion. The application of such business systems to the production of an essentially artistic structure has had the double effect of cheapening the selling price and improving the quality.

This is not the place to go into details of the organization of a modern pianoforte factory, but we may very properly devote some moments to a consideration of the main points of construction that are observable in the pianofortes of the day. Critical analysis of these points will be in order later on in the course of the present work. For the moment we shall be content with obtaining a bird's-eye view, as it were, of that which we are later to dissect and criticise.

There are to-day two distinct and prevailing types of pianoforte. These are the "upright" and the "grand." Of the once popular "square" it is unnecessary here to do more than say that the type has passed into a state of obsolescence and is fast dying out. Both structurally and tonally, it was most defective; and its popularity was due rather to the imperfect development of the other types during the period of its vogue than to any inherent advantages of its own. It has well and faithfully served its appointed time, and we may properly leave it to die in peace.

For the last thirty years in this country and for considerably longer in Europe, the upright, succeeding the square as a home instrument, has remained victorious. Its small size and great convenience, together with the surprising tonal capacity that has been developed in it in the United States, have universally commended it, and only the development of the very small grand has lately seemed to be threatening its long unchallenged supremacy.

The exterior form of an upright is familiar to all. If we strip from it all the outer appendages, and then remove the action and keys, we shall at once see that the instrument consists essentially of a sound-board and a frame, the latter partly wooden and partly metallic, upon which are stretched strings of regularly graduated lengths and thicknesses. Attached to this framing are two more or less ornate wooden erections which are denominated the "sides" of the instrument, while a horizontal wooden shelf, called the "key-bed," serves to join the sides and support the keys and their frame.

The strings of an upright are arranged vertically from the top to the bottom of the framing already described, with the exception of those which serve the bass notes. These are strung diagonally over the treble strings. It will also be observed that the strings become progressively shorter as the scale ascends until the speaking lengths at the highest notes are two inches or less. The thickness also varies directly as the length. The material of which the strings are made is cast-steel wire, and the overstrung bass strings are, in addition, covered with copper or iron wire. These strings, in order that they may be maintained at the proper tensions and in the correct positions, must be supported by suitable framing. The demands of modern construction require that the framing be most massive. We have already cast a hurried glance at it, and may now proceed to describe it in more detail. First of all, however, it is necessary to investigate the apparatus that amplifies the sound waves projected from the strings and transforms them into the pleasing tones of the pianoforte. We must, in short, examine the sound-board.

We shall have occasion later, critically to examine and discuss the resonance apparatus of the pianoforte. It is sufficient, therefore, that we glance briefly at it here, so as to familiarize ourselves with its general form and construction. The sound-board is usually constructed of a sheet of spruce fir of varying thickness and arched inwards towards the strings, the crown of the arch being at its middle portion. It carries wooden bridges, over which pass the strings and upon which the vibrations of these strings are impressed and which serve to limit their speaking lengths. The side of the sound-board, remote from the strings, is strengthened by the addition of a series of strips of hard wood called "ribs," which are tightly glued on to it.

All of this apparatus is fitted into a wooden frame technically called the "back." It consists of two horizontal beams, situated at the top and bottom of the instrument and joined together with a number of vertical wooden posts of great strength. Into this structure the sound-board is secured in such a manner as to produce the arched shape above described, and in such a manner also as to leave nearly the whole of its surface free to vibrate. The top beam of the back is covered with the "wrest-plank," a wooden block built up of crossed strips of hard maple into which are driven the tuning pins, or "wrest-pins" as they used to be called.

The whole structure is then covered by the "iron plate," which is a massive affair cast in one piece and bolted all round to the sides of the sound-board and back, and to the wrest plank at the top and the bottom beam at the bottom. This plate contains the "hitch-pins," over which are looped the waste ends of the strings, and also the iron bridge, which limits the upper extension of their speaking lengths. The strings are arranged upon this elaborate foundation, looped over the hitch-pins, passed over the sound-board—or "belly"—bridges, and thence through the bearing-bar, up to the tuning-pins.

To the sides of this structure are glued the external walls. A wooden bed for the keys is provided, and the action is secured partly to the iron plate and partly to the key-bed. The pedals are placed upon the bottom board, which is secured between the external walls or sides, and the pedals are connected with the proper parts of the action. When this has been done the construction of the instrument is essentially completed.

The various kinds of upright pianoforte do not vary greatly in size. In the United States the popular sizes vary between the extremes of four feet ten inches and four feet in height, with sufficient width to accommodate the eighty-eight notes that make up the modern compass of seven octaves and a minor third. The multitude of different scale arrangements need not be discussed here at all, nor is it necessary to enter into any investigation of the various individual arrangements and devices that different manufacturers fit to their instruments. All these things will be treated in their proper order.

The grand pianoforte has always been the favorite of the composer and the interpretative artist. In this type alone has it been possible to combine the highest qualities of tonal beauty and mechanical ingenuity. To-day the concert grands of our most eminent makers stand unsurpassed, both as mechanical structures and as musical instruments.

The most obvious dissimilarity between the grand and the upright is, of course, seen in the difference of their planes. The grand might properly be called the horizontal pianoforte. Its strings are stretched parallel to the plane of the floor and the hammers strike upwards at them from below. The second conspicuous difference is in the function of the exterior casing. We have already noted that this part of the upright is chiefly required to complete the exterior ornamentation of the structure, and secondarily to support the keys and action. The case of the grand, on the other hand, is an essential part of the resonant body of the instrument. It consists of a rim, bent to suitable shape and built up of continuous veneers, running all round in one piece and glued together at crossed grain until the desired number of layers and the proper thickness are thus obtained. The whole of what corresponds to the upright back framing, as well as the sound-board and iron plate, are rigidly built into this continuous bent rim, and thus the whole structure forms one complete resonant entity, entirely unified and interdependent. The rim is made deep enough to permit of the insertion of action and keys in the front portion, and a gap in the framing is left for the hammers to strike upwards at the strings. The wrest-plank is placed on one side of the gap and the sound-board occupies the remainder of the space on the other side. The iron plate covers the entire structure, wrest-plank included, and sustains the same relations to the instrument as in the upright. Its shape, as also that of the sound-board, is adapted to the peculiar outline of the grand, which is so aptly implied in the word "fluegel" (wing), used in Germany to designate the entire grand type.

Until a comparatively recent period the large concert size grand was practically the only type of these instruments. The revolutionary improvements initiated by the Steinways in the middle of the nineteenth century paved the way, however, for the general introduction of smaller styles. It was found possible to retain the characteristically full and rich tone of the large grand—at least to a great extent—while its inherent advantages in the matter of touch and action all combined to assure the popularity of the smaller instrument among the more critical and discriminating of the public. Doubtless, also, the remarkable change in the housing of urban populations that has been so conspicuous during the last twenty years had much to do with the general desire for an instrument that should be less common than the ordinary upright and that should at the same time be less cumbersome than the full-sized grand. A powerful incentive was therefore given to manufacturers to strive towards the perfecting of the small types, and we cannot deny that they have succeeded in a remarkable manner.

It is true that there exists today a tendency to cut the size of these small grands down to really impossible proportions. There is a limit to the cutting down process; and it is apparent to the observer that more than one maker is endeavoring to obtain a true grand tone from a sound-board area and from string lengths that are such as entirely to prohibit the attainment of this desirable goal. Of course, it may be retorted that the term "true grand tone" is subject to variations of definition. It may even be plausibly said that tone of any kind is too intangible a thing to be limited by any definitions. Nevertheless, it would seem that there is a very decided limit, and that when we arrive at the point where it is no longer possible to obtain the fullness, richness and volume of tone that we are accustomed to accept as the distinguishing characteristic of the grand pianoforte, then, indeed, we no longer have a true grand. Other instruments may have the outline and the action of a grand, but if they have not the proper sound-board area and string length, then they are merely (if we may perpetrate a bull) "horizontal uprights."

The very general description that we have thus given of the two prevailing types of pianoforte has not been intended to serve as more than what it so obviously is—a rapid bird's-eye view of the instruments as they appear to the casual observer. The reader may thus prepare himself for the more definite and critical investigation that is now about to be begun.

CHAPTER IV.
ACOUSTICAL LAWS OF SOUNDING STRINGS.

Sound is an impression produced upon the brain through the ear by the motion of air particles excited by an external body. In the transmission of sound from the vibrating or "sonorous" body to the ear it is motion that is transferred and not the substance of the air itself. In the same way there can be no sensation of sound without the interposition of an elastic fluid such as air or water, and the production of sound in a vacuum is, therefore, impossible.

Sound, in short, has no objective existence. We know it simply as a sensation, primarily caused by certain physical processes, the nature of which is comparatively familiar to us. We are aware of all that goes on between a sounding body and the ear, but we know nothing of the processes whereby these physical motions are transformed until they become, within the brain, sensations of musical sound or of noise.

While so much of mystery clouds our conception of the nature of sound, we may take comfort in the knowledge that to penetrate the enigma is by no means necessary. Not even the musician requires such transcendent knowledge. To the student of musical craftsmanship it is equally non-essential. It is well, however, to recognize the fact that as soon as we leave the sure ground of physical investigation, we become lost in impenetrable mystery and find ourselves face to face with the ancient, yet ever new, questions of our origin and destination. When we reflect upon the essentially spiritual and unearthly influence of music, we cannot but feel that, in the making of instruments to serve this art, we are ourselves assisting, however blindly, at a more than Eleusinian mystery.

The ear easily distinguishes between musical and non-musical sounds. Nor does it fail to recognize differences in relative loudness or softness of any given musical sound. Again, the relative degree of acuteness or gravity is distinguished, and, lastly, the quality of the same musical note when played upon two different instruments or when sung by two different voices is no less easily observed.

Now we have first to ask ourselves in what the difference between musical and non-musical sounds consists. We may say that a musical sound is produced by regularly recurring motions of the sounding body communicated to the air; or, more technically, a musical sound may be defined as a sound produced by periodical vibrations. This may be proved by holding a piece of cardboard against a rapidly revolving toothed wheel.

As long as the revolutions of the wheel are performed at a comparatively slow speed the noise produced by the impact of the cardboard is broken and disjointed; but as the wheel is caused to revolve with greater rapidity the noise becomes gradually continuous and assumes a definite pitch. By increasing the speed of the wheel we cause a higher pitched musical sound to be produced. Now, if we arrange a second card and wheel and cause them to be set in motion together with the first we shall find that when the two wheels are revolved at the same speed, they produce sounds of the same pitch. Thus it is apparent that the pitch of a musical sound depends upon the speed of vibration, or upon the number of vibrations per second. Without going too deeply into technicalities it may be said that similar experiments have enabled investigators to determine the behavior of sonorous bodies in reference to all the other conditions that pertain to them. Thus, in the case of strings such as are used in the pianoforte, we are in possession of facts that make it possible for us to state accurately the pitches that will pertain to strings of given lengths, densities and thicknesses, which are stretched at given tensions. It is unnecessary to go into details of the precise methods employed to demonstrate these laws, and it will be quite sufficient to quote the laws themselves. The reader is therefore invited to note carefully that:

1. The number of vibrations of a string is inversely proportional to the length of the string.

2. The pitch of a musical sound is proportional to the number of vibrations per second; the greater the number of vibrations, the higher the pitch.

3. The number of vibrations per second of a string is proportional to the square root of its tension. That is to say, if a string is stretched with a weight of one pound it will give forth a sound one octave lower than the sound that it would emit if stretched with a weight of four pounds.

4. The number of vibrations of a string varies inversely as the thickness of the string. So that if there are two strings of the same material and length and subjected to the same tension, and if the diameter of the first is twice the diameter of the second, the first will produce one-half as many vibrations as the second.

5. The number of vibrations per second of a string varies inversely as the square root of its density. Thus, if one string has four times the density of another, the first will produce one-half as many vibrations as the second.

In addition to these valuable laws, there are certain others which have reference to the actual musical sounds produced by strings. By means of them we know the relative proportions of the strings that will, other things being equal, give the various notes of the musical scale. If a perfect musical string be stretched and excited into vibration it will be found that an exact octave above the note that the whole string gives out may be produced by dividing the string at its precise middle point and causing one of the halves to vibrate. Now we have already noted that the number of vibrations of a string is proportional to its length, and it is therefore obvious that the halves of the given string each have double the number of vibrations of the whole, and that, consequently, the octave to a note is produced by either twice or half the number of vibrations that suffice to produce the given note.

Carrying the experiment further, we may, by dividing the given string at other points on its surface, obtain all the other notes of the musical scale. It will not be necessary to repeat the explanation in each case, and the reader will have no difficulty in comprehending the following table, which gives the relative string length required to produce the eight notes of the diatonic scale of C major, taking the length of the complete string that gives the keynote as 1, and considering all other pertinent conditions to remain equal:

C	D	E	F	G	A	B	C
1	8/9	4/5	3/4	2/3	3/5	8/15	1/2
Keynote	2d	3d	4th	5th	6th	7th	Octave

At first sight it might appear that the above data ought to give us all necessary information in regard to the phenomena of vibrating strings. Undoubtedly, the difficulties that surround the pianoforte designer would have little power to cause worry if there were nothing more to learn. Our troubles, however, are but just now beginning, and the difficulties that still exist are greater than any that we have yet investigated. These difficulties have their origin in the *nature* of the sounds that are emitted by musical strings.

While we have been investigating the relative vibration speeds and pitches that pertain to the strings under various conditions, we have not as yet paid attention to any other difficulties that might have their origin under entirely different circumstances. There are, however, certain highly important phenomena which are determined by the nature of the strings themselves, irrespective of all other conditions. These phenomena affect the constitution of such sounds as any musical string may produce. Sounds produced through the agency of musical strings are not and cannot be simple sounds. And this peculiarity arises from the fact that such strings in common with most other agencies for the production of musical sounds are incapable of performing perfectly simple vibrations. If a string vibrated as a whole uniformly and all the time, its motions might be compared to the rhythmic swing of a pendulum, and the sounds that it emitted would be absolutely simple and absolutely pure. The fact, however, is that this never occurs. No string ever vibrates as a whole without simultaneously vibrating in segments, which are aliquot parts of the whole. These segments, when thus vibrating, give out the sounds that pertain to them according to their relative lengths; while the vibration of the whole length of the string, at the same time, causes the production of the sound proper to it, which is called the "prime" or "fundamental" tone. The sounds produced by the simultaneously vibrating segments are called "partial tones" or "upper partials." In the case of sounding strings, such as we are now investigating, the partials follow each other in arithmetical progression and are produced by the vibrating of segments the proportions of which may be expressed by the harmonic series 1, ½, ⅓, ¼, ⅕, ⅙, ⅐, ⅛, ⅑, and so on ad infinitum. Now, if we examine this series we shall see that the lower of the partial tones that are represented by the various fractions must bear distinct harmonic relations to the fundamental tone. It will simultaneously be observed, however, that as the series is continued, the fractional quantities become uniformly smaller, and the difference between any pair of them (for the same reason) is smaller as the position of the given pair is more remote from unity. Naturally, this means that the partial tones represented by such fractional quantities are separated by continually decreasing intervals. If the process is carried far enough, the time comes when the interval of separation is less than a semitone. Clearly, then, partial tones in this condition can bear no proper harmonic relation to the fundamental tone. They are, in fact, dissonant.

Here, then, we come upon a fact that has a very wide bearing. It is a demonstrated acoustical truth that tone quality depends upon the number and intensity of the partial tones that accompany the fundamental during the sounding of any musical note. If, through any cause, these high and dissonant partials are excited into undue prominence, they may, and do, exercise a profound and maleficent influence upon the quality of musical sounds. We shall later have occasion to confirm the truth of this statement, and we shall learn, in the course of our investigation, fully to appreciate its importance in the practical problems of pianoforte design.

For the purpose of assisting the reader in the comprehension of the above argument, the following table is given, showing the order of succession and pitch of the partial tones of the note C (second line below the staff in the bass clef). Taking the pitch of the octave above middle C, for convenience of calculation, as 512 vibrations per second, this gives us 64 for the C in question.

NAME OF NOTE	C1	C2	G2	C3	E3	G3	B♭3	C4	D4	E4	F♯4	G4	A4	B♭4	B♮4	C5
ORDER OF SUCCESSION	1	2	3	4	5	6	7	8	9	10	11	12	13	14	15	16
VIBRATION PER SECOND	64	128	192	256	320	384	448	512	576	640	704	768	832	896	960	1024

It should be observed that the seventh, eleventh and fourteenth partials and their multiples cannot more than approximately be indicated in musical notation, as they do not exactly correspond to the notes that are written to represent them. We are obliged to be content with an approximation to the true pitch of these partials and the notation given here is as near as it is possible to approach.

A brief consideration of the facts thus presented will convince the reader that a combination of any fundamental tone with its first eight partials will produce a relatively harmonious effect. At the same time we must observe that this harmoniousness is more and more obliterated as the higher partials are permitted to sound simultaneously with the others. In fact, it may be said that, although we can not and must not eliminate the dissonant partials altogether, we should attempt to cause the strings to vibrate with entire freedom only as far as concerns the first eight partials, and less freely as far as concerns the others.

Now, in what manner can this desirable end be attained? To answer this question we must first discover what pre-disposing causes, if any, exist towards the favoring of any combination of partials at the expense of any other.

In speaking of the automatic sub-division of a string into vibrating segments, we omitted, at the time, to make mention of a fact which should, however, be obvious to the reader; namely, that the various points at which the sub-division occur are themselves motionless.

It would be more correct, perhaps, to say "apparently motionless"; for, of course, if these dividing points or "nodes," as they are called, were entirely without motion, the formation of the vibrating segments would be impossible. In most cases, however, the "amplitude" or length of swing of the nodes when in motion is very much smaller than the amplitude of vibration of the segments. Consequently, as the vibration of the segments of a string is itself ordinarily invisible, the motion of the nodes may be considered as inappreciable.

Now, these nodes exercise considerable influence upon the problems that we are considering. For example, according to the researches of Young, it appears that when a string is struck at any point all those partials are obliterated that have their nodes at that point. Curiously enough, however, it has since been found in the case of the pianoforte, that those upper partials are not *necessarily* eliminated that have their nodes at the striking point.

Undoubtedly, however, a properly chosen node provides the best possible striking point, since its selection permits the operation of its tendency to suppress those particular partials that have their nodes at the same place.

A consideration of the phenomena already observed has caused us to perceive that the highest partials of the compound tone produced by a musical string do not bear precise harmonic relations to the prime tone. As the successive sub-divisions of the string approach closer and closer to each other, the tones thus generated are seen to be distant by proportionately less intervals, until at length they cease to have a close similarity to any tone of the musical scale. Consequently, as was said before, they exercise a generally harsh and dissonant influence upon the nature of the compound tone. We have already concluded that, broadly speaking, we should aim to eliminate these dissonant partials and, conversely, to favor the prominence of those which are more nearly harmonic. The reasoning which has served to lead us to this conclusion may profitably be carried a step further. If the highest partials are non-harmonic, it is obvious that their presence or absence, their prominence or the reverse, must necessarily exercise much influence upon the actual quality of a musical sound; upon the individual color which different generating agencies impart to the same musical note; in effect, upon all the numerous gradations of what we are accustomed to call harshness, hollowness or mellowness of tonal quality.

This inevitable conclusion has been fully substantiated by the results of experiment. The labors of Helmholtz and Koenig have demonstrated conclusively that the quality of a musical sound depends upon the number and intensity of the partial tones that accompany the fundamental. Thus the mystery of the individual tone coloring that distinguishes the voices of different musical instruments or of different persons is transferred from the realm of psychology to that of science. In fine, it becomes clear that if we can govern the number of the segments into which a vibrating string divides itself, and if we can also control the amplitude of vibration of these segments, we shall find it possible to alter the tone quality of a musical instrument at our pleasure.

It has already been observed that the generation of certain partial tones is assisted or retarded as the position of the striking point on a string is changed. It may not be out of place to note that the various other methods of exciting a string, such as plucking, bowing, etc., permit the production of equally variable effects as the points at which they operate are changed. Our inquiry, however, is confined to the pianoforte, and we shall therefore continue to limit ourselves to the cases of pianoforte strings as struck by the usual hammers.

The matter of choosing a proper striking point was first systematically investigated by John Broadwood, founder of the celebrated house of that name, in the early part of the nineteenth century. Until that time the pianoforte makers had, apparently, paid no attention to this important problem and had been content to follow in the steps of the builders of harpsichords and spinets. Examination of any of the instruments that are direct ancestors of the pianoforte will show that the strings are struck, indifferently, at any point from one-tenth to one-half of the speaking length. The only exceptions appear to be those clavichords in which the strings are all of the same length and in which the tangents on the keys impinge upon the strings at different fixed points to give the corresponding notes of the scale. Since the time of Broadwood, however, the vast importance of correctness in this particular has come to be recognized with more or less unanimity.

The investigations undertaken by this eminent maker convinced him that the ideal striking point lay between one-seventh and one-ninth of the speaking length of the string. Now, our investigations have shown us that the most harmonious and agreeable compound tone is that which is formed by the combination of the first eight partials. It would seem, therefore, that one-eighth of the speaking length would be more correct than the approximation that was arrived at by Broadwood. Theoretically, indeed, the latter is nearer to the ideal point; is, in fact, the ideal point. For obvious mechanical reasons, however, it is usually impossible to hit this point with exactitude, and the approximation suggested and used by Broadwood has been proved, by the practice of the best makers, to offer the nearest practical solution.

We may, then, lay it down as a rule to be followed that a point as nearly as possible midway between one-seventh and one-ninth of the speaking length of the string should be chosen and adhered to as the proper place where the blow of the hammer should be struck. If this rule be faithfully followed the greatest obstacle to purity of tone is removed and the most harmonious and agreeable combination of partials is in a fair way to be secured. Nevertheless, it is necessary to make an exception for the highest notes on the piano. Practical experience has shown that one-tenth is a better striking point for the very highest and shortest strings.

Thus we have been able to enunciate and discuss the principal laws that govern the activities of sounding strings, particularly those of the pianoforte. As the argument is developed, it will often appear that the theoretical exactitude of the rules here laid down must be modified in practice. Such a condition is always inevitable as between a body of laws and the application thereof. It will be found, however, that the variations to be recorded are not generally very important, and the reader will be well advised to make the rules enunciated in this chapter his continual leaning post and guide.

The most conspicuous difference is, perhaps, that which exists between the theoretical and practical results of halving string lengths to obtain octaves. In practice it is found that pianoforte strings generally sound a little flat of the octave when divided at exactly the middle point. But the variation is the fault of the steel wire and not of the rule.

CHAPTER V.
THE MUSICAL SCALE AND MUSICAL INTONATION.

We have now considered as much of the phenomena of musical sounds as may be considered to have a bearing upon the purpose of our investigations. We may then devote some space to the matter of the expression of musical ideas, and the intonation which has been devised in order to reduce the mental products of composers to the limitations of musical instruments. Music is expressed through the medium of a scale of tones, all of which bear definite relations to each other as to pitch. The "diatonic scale," which is the foundation of musical intonation, is composed of a series of eight tones which are named after letters of the alphabet, the last tone having the same name as, and being the octave to, the first. The frequencies of these tones always bear the same ratios, one to another, whatever may be their positions within the compass of any instrument. Now, considering the frequency of the first tone to be unity, the frequencies of the others are in the following proportions:

C	D	E	F	G	A	B	C
1	$9/8$	$5/4$	$4/3$	$3/2$	$5/3$	$15/8$	2

If we now divide these proportionate numbers each by the other we have the proportionate intervals that separate them. Doing this, we have the following result:

C	D	E	F	G	A	B	C
	$9/8$	$10/9$	$16/15$	$9/8$	$10/9$	$9/8$	$16/15$

Now, it will be observed that we have in the above table three different kinds of interval represented by the three ratios, $9/8$, $10/9$ and $16/15$. The first of these is called the major tone and the second the minor tone, while the third is known as the diatonic semitone. Following out these ratios, we may obtain the frequencies of any diatonic series. We shall choose the scale of which C 528 is the key-note. Its frequencies are as follows:

C	D	E	F	G	A	B	C
1	$9/8$	$5/4$	$4/3$	$3/2$	$5/3$	$15/8$	$2/1$
528	594	660	704	792	880	990	1056

Knowing as we do the ratios and frequencies already calculated, it is obvious that we may similarly calculate the ratios and frequencies for the diatonic scale, of which any given tone is the tonic or key-note. Before doing this, however, it is well for us to remember that the diatonic scale is not adequate to all the requirements of music. Musicians have found it necessary to interpolate other sounds in between those which form the diatonic progression. The reason for this is that music, in order that it may have the greatest possible freedom of expression, must be written in a larger number of keys, and must contain more distinct sounds than the diatonic scale is able to afford. For these and other cognate reasons the chromatic scale was introduced. The addition of five chromatic semitones, obtained by taking the difference between a minor tone and a diatonic semitone, gives the chromatic scale thirteen semitones from key-note to octave. Unfortunately, however, the same number of keys upon the pianoforte cannot provide us with thirteen pure chromatic sounds in every key. This may be demonstrated as follows: The ratio of a chromatic semitone is $25/24$. The sharp of C 528 is, therefore, 550. But in the diatonic scale of D (the major second in scale of C), C sharp has a frequency of 1113 ¾. The octave below this latter sound is the C sharp, which is one chromatic semitone above C 528. We know the frequency of the latter to be 550. The frequency of the octave below C sharp, 1113 ¾, ought, therefore, to be 550. But we know that the octave below any given note has a frequency that is one-half that of the given note. Now, one-half of 1113 ¾ is 556 ⅞. Therefore, we see that there is a difference of 6 ⅞ vibrations per second between the C sharp that is a chromatic semitone above C 528 and the C sharp that is the octave below the major seventh of the scale of D, and which ought to be the same sound, as it is in the same position on the key-board as the former. By carrying the same investigation further we are enabled to perceive that sounds of the same name are not identical when played in different keys, or, rather, that the same name does not imply that the sound so denoted means the same thing when it is considered in its relation to any tonic different to that to which it was first related. There is another difficulty also that confronts us in the problem of playing pure sounds upon the pianoforte; that instrument, as we know, does not provide us with different keys for the sharp of one sound and the flat of the sound next above it. There is a general belief that C sharp, for example, and D flat are identical. But this is not so. The flat of D is a chromatic semitone below that note, while the sharp of C is the same interval above the latter. By referring to our former calculations it will be seen that the chromatic semitone ratio is $25/24$. The sharp of C is, therefore, obtained by multiplying the frequency of C by $25/24$, and the flat of D is likewise evolved by an inverse process, namely, by dividing the frequency of D by the same ratio. This is equivalent to adding a chromatic semitone to C and subtracting the same from D. If we take the notes C and D from the scale of C 528, we have the frequencies of C and D as 528 and 594 respectively. Effecting the multiplication and division as above we see that C sharp has a frequency of

550, while that of D flat is 570 6/25. That is to say that these two notes differ by no less than 20 6/25 vibrations per second.

It thus becomes obvious that the expression of all the sounds within the compass of an octave, in such a manner that absolutely correct sounds in every key may be obtained, is a problem that calls for more sounds than are provided by the pianoforte. As a correct understanding of this most important subject is essential, a somewhat elaborate treatment of it will be given here. The reader who takes the pains to master the true inwardness of the problem of musical intonation will have an insight into the matter which few pianoforte makers or musicians possess.

"Just intonation" is the name given to that system whereby we are enabled to command the expression of all the sounds that are required to be heard within the compass of an octave in order that the degrees of each and every possible scale may be correctly and exactly rendered. It is not difficult to see that performers upon instruments which do not have fixed tones should have no difficulty in adjusting the intonation of every tone to correspond with the variations in pitch required by the different positions in the scale that such tones may occupy. Experiments have, in fact, been carried out with violinists and it has been shown that artists upon this instrument do naturally play the true diatonic and chromatic intervals when left to themselves and when not forced to adjust their intonation to that of fixed tone instruments.

In order to show with accuracy the total number of different sounds that are required to produce "just intonation" in every possible key the reader is invited to consider the following table, which shows the smallest possible number of sounds that will give the true diatonic intervals in twelve keys. The first note in each row is the key-note and the last the octave thereto. The frequencies of those key-notes that are not represented in the first scale (that of C) have been calculated as follows:

- The key-note to scale of B-flat is the perfect fourth to key-note of scale F.

- The key-note to scale of E-flat is the perfect fourth to key-note of scale B-flat

- The key-note to scale of F-sharp is the octave below major seventh of scale G.

- The key-note to scale of G-sharp is the octave below major seventh of scale A.

- The key-note to scale of C-sharp is the octave below major seventh of scale D.

We therefore have the following results:

C 528	D 594	E 660	F 704	G 792	A 880	B 990	C 1056
C-sharp 556 7/8	D-sharp 626 3/64	E-sharp 696 3/32	F-sharp 742 1/2	G-sharp 835 5/16	A-sharp 928 1/8	B-sharp 1044 9/64	C-sharp 113 3/4
D 594	E 668 1/4	F-sharp 742 1/2	G 792	A 881	B 990	C-sharp 1113 3/4	D 1188
E-flat 625 4/9	F 703 45/72	G 781 34/36	A-flat 833 25/27	B-flat 938 1/18	C 1042 11/27	D 1172 59/72	E-flat 1250 8/9
E 660	F-sharp 742 1/2	G-sharp 825	A 880	B 990	C-sharp 1100	D-sharp 1237 1/2	E 1320
F 704	G 792	A 880	B-flat 938 2/3	C 1056	D 1173 1/3	E 1320	F 1408
F-sharp 742 1/2	G-sharp 835 5/16	A-sharp 928 1/8	B 990	C-sharp 1113 3/4	D-sharp 1237 1/3	E-sharp 1392 3/15	F-sharp 1492
G 704	A 792	B 880	C 938	D 1056	E 1173	F-sharp 1320	G 1408
G-sharp 825	A-sharp 928 1/8	B-sharp 1031 3/4	C-sharp 1100	D-sharp 1237 1/2	E-sharp 1375	Fx 1546 1/8	G-sharp 1650
A 880	B 990	C-sharp 1100	D 1173 1/3	E 1320	F-sharp 1466 2/3	G-sharp 1650	A 1760
B-flat 938 2/3	C 1056	D 1173 1/6	E-flat 1258 8/9	F 1408	G 1564 4/9	A 1760	B-flat 1877 1/3
B 990	C-sharp 1113 3/4	D-sharp 1237 1/2	E 1320	F-sharp 1485	G-sharp 1650	A-sharp 1856 1/4	B 1980

C 528	D 594	E 660	F 704	G 792	A 880	B 990	C 1056
C-sharp 556 7/8	D-sharp 626 3/64	E-sharp 696 3/32	F-sharp 742 1/2	G-sharp 835 5/16	A-sharp 928 1/8	B-sharp 1044 9/64	C-sharp 113 3/4
D 594	E 668 1/4	F-sharp 742 1/2	G 792	A 881	B 990	C-sharp 1113 3/4	D 1188
E-flat 625 4/9	F 703 45/72	G 781 34/36	A-flat 833 25/27	B-flat 938 1/18	C 1042 11/27	D 1172 59/72	E-flat 1250 8/9
E 660	F-sharp 742 1/2	G-sharp 825	A 880	B 990	C-sharp 1100	D-sharp 1237 1/2	E 1320

F 704	G 792	A 880	B-flat 938 ⅔	C 1056	D 1173 ⅓	E 1320	F 1408
F-sharp 742 ½	G-sharp 835 5/16	A-sharp 928 ⅛	B 990	C-sharp 1113 ¾	D-sharp 1237 ⅓	E-sharp 1392 3/15	F-sharp 1492
G 704	A 792	B 880	C 938	D 1056	E 1173	F-sharp 1320	G 1408
G-sharp 825	A-sharp 928 ⅛	B-sharp 1031 ¾	C-sharp 1100	D-sharp 1237 ½	E-sharp 1375	Fx 1546 ⅛	G-sharp 1650
A 880	B 990	C-sharp 1100	D 1173 ⅓	E 1320	F-sharp 1466 ⅔	G-sharp 1650	A 1760
B-flat 938 ⅔	C 1056	D 1173 ⅙	E-flat 1258 8/9	F 1408	G 1564 4/9	A 1760	B-flat 1877 ⅓
B 990	C-sharp 1113 ¾	D-sharp 1237 ½	E 1320	F-sharp 1485	G-sharp 1650	A-sharp 1856 ¼	B 1980

In order that the different sounds may more easily be separated, they have been collated in linear progression, together with their frequencies and the scales in which they or their octaves appear:

1.	The sound C	= 528	Appears in the scales of	C, F, G, B-flat.
2.	" C	= 521 11/54		E-flat
3.	" C-sharp	= 556 ⅞		D, B, F-sharp, C-sharp
4.	" C-sharp	= 550		A, E, G-sharp
5.	" D	= 594		C-G
6.	" D	= 586 ⅔		A, F, B-flat, E-flat
7.	" D-sharp	= 618 ¾		E, B, F-sharp, G-sharp
8.	" D-sharp	= 626 31/64		C-sharp.

9.	"	E-flat	= 625 4/9		B-flat
10.	"	E	= 660		C, G, A, E, B-flat
11.	"	E	= 668 1/4		D
12.	"	E-sharp	= 696 3/32		F-sharp, C-sharp
13.	"	E-sharp	= 687 1/2		G-sharp.
14.	"	F	= 704		C, F, B-flat
15.	"	F-sharp	= 742 1/2		G, D, E, B, F-sharp, C-sharp
16.	"	F-sharp	= 753 1/3		A
17.	"	G	= 792		C, D, F, G
18.	"	G	= 782 4/13		B-flat
19.	"	G	= 781 34/36		E-flat
20.	"	Fx	= 773 6/16		G-sharp
21.	"	G-sharp	= 825		A, E, B, G-sharp
22.	"	G-sharp	= 835 5/16		F-sharp, C-sharp
23.	"	A-flat	= 833 25/27		E-flat
24.	"	A	= 880		C, E, F, A
25.	"	A	= 881		D
26.	"	A	= 891		G

27.	" sharp	A-	= 928 ⅛			B, F-sharp, C-sharp, G-sharp
28.	" flat	B-	= 938 ⅔			F, B-flat, E-flat
29.	"	B	= 990			C, G, D, A, E, B, F-sharp
30.	" sharp	B-	= 1031 ¼			G-sharp
31.	" sharp	B-	= 1044 ⁸⁄₆₄			C-sharp

Thus we see that thirty-one different sounds are required to give the true diatonic intervals in only twelve keys. But it is not necessary to remind the reader that there are more keys than these used in music. We have, in fact, not yet considered the keys of A flat, D flat and G flat. The frequencies of the keynotes of these scales have been calculated as follows:

- A-flat is the perfect fourth to E-flat, which as calculated above = 625 therefore A-flat = 833 $^{25}/_{27}$.

- D-flat is the perfect fourth to A-flat, which as calculated above = 833 $^{25}/_{27}$ therefore D-flat = 555 $^{154}/_{162}$.

- G-flat is the perfect fourth to D-flat, which as calculated above = 555 $^{154}/_{162}$ therefore G-flat = 741 $^{130}/_{486}$.

We are therefore able to construct these following additional scales:

A-flat	B-flat	C	D-flat	E-flat	F	G	A-flat
833 $^{25}/_{27}$	938 $^{26}/_{316}$	1042 $^{73}/_{236}$	1111 $^{73}/_{81}$	1250 $^{8}/_{9}$	1389 $^{21}/_{52}$	1563 $^{132}/_{216}$	1666 $^{50}/_{54}$
D-flat	E-flat	F	G-flat	A-flat	B-flat	C	D-flat
555 $^{154}/_{162}$	624 $^{640}/_{1290}$	694 $^{365}/_{648}$	741 $^{130}/_{486}$	833 $^{150}/_{162}$	926 $^{284}/_{486}$	1042 $^{528}/_{1296}$	1111 $^{146}/_{152}$
G-flat	A-flat	B-flat	C-flat	D-flat	E-flat	F	G-flat
741 $^{130}/_{486}$	823 $^{3600}/_{3888}$	926 $^{1136}/_{1944}$	988 $^{520}/_{1458}$	1111 $^{308}/_{456}$	1285 $^{650}/_{1458}$	1389 $^{1408}/_{3088}$	1482 $^{260}/_{486}$

A-flat 833 $25/27$	B-flat 938 $26/316$	C 1042 $73/236$	D-flat 1111 $73/81$	E-flat 1250 $8/9$	F 1389 $21/52$	G 1563 $132/216$	A-flat 1666 $50/54$
D-flat 555 $154/162$	E-flat 624 $640/1290$	F 694 $365/648$	G-flat 741 $130/486$	A-flat 833 $150/162$	B-flat 926 $284/486$	C 1042 $528/1296$	D-flat 1111 $146/152$
G-flat 741 $130/486$	A-flat 823 $3600/3888$	B-flat 926 $1136/1944$	C-flat 988 $520/1458$	D-flat 1111 $308/456$	E-flat 1285 $650/1458$	F 1389 $1408/3088$	G-flat 1482 $260/486$

By examining the last table the reader will perceive that we have obtained fourteen new sounds. They are shown graphically in this manner:

- In the scale of A-flat the new sounds are B-flat, C, D-flat, F and G.
- In the scale of D-flat the new sounds are E-flat, F, G-flat, and A-flat.
- In the scale of G-flat the new sounds are A-flat, C-flat, D-flat, E-flat and F.

None of these sounds had been obtained in the scales given before and, consequently, we have to consider that there are fourteen more sounds to be added to the thirty-one that we have already found.

The above calculations would suffice to provide us with the diatonic intervals in all the keys that are used in music. Harmony demands, however, certain other intervals. These are minor thirds, minor sevenths, dominant sevenths and minor sixths. Accordingly, if we desire to probe the matter of just intonation to its depths, we must calculate the sounds that are required to make up these intervals in such scales as are now without them. Examining the tables already prepared, we find that there are wanting the following members:

- Minor thirds to the key-notes of the scales C, D, E-flat, F, G, B-flat, A-flat, D-flat, G-flat.
- Minor sixths to the key-notes of the scale C, E-flat, B-flat, A-flat, G-flat, and D-flat.
- Dominant sevenths to the key-notes of the scales E-flat, F and B-flat.

- Minor sevenths to the key-notes of the scales A-flat, D-flat, and G-flat.

We shall have no difficulty in calculating the frequencies of the required notes by the same processes that we have followed heretofore.

Key-notes—								
C 528	D 594	E-flat 625 $4/9$	F 704	G 792	B-flat 938 $2/3$	A-flat 833 $25/27$	D-flat 555 $146/152$	G-flat 741 $124/486$
Minor thirds—$6/5$ Ratio								
E-flat 633 $3/5$	F 712 $4/5$	G-flat 750 $4/55$	A-flat 844 $4/5$	B-flat 950 $2/5$	D-flat 1125 $11/15$	C-flat 1000 $106/135$	F-flat 667 $66/810$	B double flat 889 $1330/2430$
Minor sixths—$8/5$ Ratio								
A-flat 841 $4/5$		C-flat 1000 $32/45$			G-flat 1501 $13/15$	F-flat 667 $38/276$	B double flat 889 $358/810$	E double flat 593 $10/2400$
Dominant sevenths—$16/9$ Ratio								
		D-flat 1111 $80/81$	E-flat 1251 $5/9$		A-flat 1668 $20/27$			
Minor sevenths—$9/5$ Ratio								
						G-flat 741 $64/243$	C-flat 988 $359/810$	F-flat 658 $2908/4374$

Key-notes—								
C 528	D 594	E-flat 625 $4/9$	F 704	G 792	B-flat 938 $2/3$	A-flat 833 $25/27$	D-flat 555 $146/152$	G-flat 741 $124/486$
Minor thirds—$6/5$ Ratio								
E-flat 633 $3/5$	F 712 $4/5$	G-flat 750 $4/55$	A-flat 844 $4/5$	B-flat 950 $2/5$	D-flat 1125 $11/15$	C-flat 1000 $106/135$	F-flat 667 $66/810$	B double flat 889 $1330/2430$
Minor sixths—$8/5$ Ratio								
A-flat 841 $4/5$		C-flat 1000 $32/45$			G-flat 1501 $13/15$	F-flat 667 $38/276$	B double flat 889 $358/810$	E double flat 593 $10/2400$

	Dominant sevenths—$^{16}/_9$ Ratio					
	D-flat 1111 $^{80}/_{81}$	E-flat 1251 $^5/_9$		A-flat 1668 $^{20}/_{27}$		
				Minor sevenths—$^9/_5$ Ratio		
				G-flat 741 $^{64}/_{243}$	C-flat 988 $^{359}/_{810}$	F-flat 658 $^{2908}/_{4374}$

The result of these calculations may now be collated and summarized. We find that there are no less than sixty-six separate sounds required for the production of the necessary intervals in all the possible scales. These sounds are thus classified:

Different sounds in twelve diatonic scales	31
Sounds wanting to complete the diatonic scales of A-flat, D-flat, G-flat	14
Minor thirds wanting in scales of C, E-flat, F, G, B-flat	6
Minor sixths wanting in scales of C, E-flat, and B-flat	3
Dominant sevenths wanting in scales of E-flat, F and B-flat	3
Minor thirds wanting in scales of A-flat, D-flat and G-flat	3
Minor sixths wanting in scales of A-flat, D-flat and G-flat	3
Minor sevenths wanting in scales of A-flat, D-flat and G-flat	3
Total number of sounds in an octave	66

Now the obvious conclusion to be drawn from this analysis is that the true sounds of the just musical scales are very different from any that we hear upon the pianoforte. Indeed, we may properly carry the reasoning a step further. If the expression of all the degrees of the true musical scales requires this formidable array of sounds, then surely, the sounds that are produced upon the piano are not all of the required true sounds, but are totally unlike any of them. For it is evident that if the sixty-six true sounds within the compass of an octave have to be reduced to the thirteen that are found upon the pianoforte, the process of compression to which the former must be subjected will force the latter into the position of so many compromises. In fact, with the exception of the standard tone from which all calculations and all tuning must start, and its octaves, there is no tone upon the piano, as it is now tuned, which is identical with any sound of the justly tuned scale. The process to which we have alluded, and which is necessary to secure to the piano and all other instruments with fixed tones the ability to perform music in all keys which are desired for the proper expression of the composers' ideas, is called temperament. Upon the skill and cunning with which this compromise with natural laws is effected depends the whole beauty of, and the whole of our pleasure in, music as we are accustomed to hear it. It would be vain to pretend that tempered intonation is preferable to that which is pure and just, but it is equally vain and foolish to decry the accepted system of temperament until the mechanical skill of manufacturers of musical instruments and the taste of performers have risen to the point of appreciating the beauties of pure intonation and of devising mechanical means of attaining it. Until that time arrives we must fain be content to accept what we have and make the best of it. There have, of course, been attempts to provide instruments that could be used to give the pure intervals in every key, but they have been invariably failures. Most of them have been forced to depend upon tempered intonation to a certain extent, while others have been mechanically impossible.

In any case we must remember that the pianoforte, as at present constructed and played, depends entirely upon an equally tempered intonation. So strongly has the pianoforte entrenched itself in popular favor, indeed, that music and tempered intonation have become, to most people, exactly synonymous. It is proper that we should be able to draw true distinctions, however, as the practical work of piano building ought to be largely guided by the considerations induced from the necessity and fact of temperament.

CHAPTER VI.
THE EQUAL TEMPERAMENT.

As was suggested in the last chapter, it becomes necessary to effect a compromise between the demands of true musical intonation and the limitations of musical instruments, in order that the performance of music may be made practicable. The equal temperament, now universally employed, has only risen to its present commanding position within the last century. It seems to have been first used by Johann Sebastian Bach. Händel did not know it, and it struggled throughout the whole of the eighteenth century with the mean-tone system.

Temperament systems were, however, invented and used long before this period. Pythagoras, the Greek pre-Christian philosopher, was one of the earliest experimenters along these lines. The method that he devised has come down to us, and we are thus able to see wherein lies the difference between it and the modern diatonic scale. Without going into too much detail, we may note that the Pythagorean system recognizes only two intervals; namely, the tone and semitone. The diatonic scale, as we know, has a major tone, a minor tone and a diatonic semitone. The Pythagorean scale contemplates perfect fifths and sharped thirds, and is incapable of the effects of modern harmony.

The next attempt to adapt the necessary compromise in the interests of practical music was introduced after the modern diatonic scale had become the standard method of octave-division; that is to say, some time in the fifteenth century. It has been variously called the "mean-tone," "mesotonic" and "vulgar" temperament. In this method the tone is a mean or average between the major and minor tones of the diatonic scale. The fifths are all flattened, while the thirds are justly tuned. Such a system possesses both advantages and disadvantages. On the one hand, the nearer and more frequently used scales are purer and more agreeable; on the other hand, the remoter scales are exceedingly dissonant; so much so, in fact, that they cannot be employed with pleasure to either the performer or the hearer. So long, however, as the music is written in the commoner scales the mean-tone temperament, possessing the great advantage over other methods of having pure thirds, is far more agreeable to the ear. In fact, up till a few years ago it was not uncommon to find organs in village churches in Europe that were still tuned according to this system. The mean-tone system first made harmony, as we understand it, practicable, but as the knowledge and imagination of composers widened, the desire naturally arose to take advantage of the greater powers for harmony that could alone be afforded by the unrestricted possession of all possible scales. A substitute for the mean-tone system had, therefore, to be found, and thus arose the modern and accepted method, universally known as the Equal Temperament. By this method, which is at the present time universal, the octave is divided into thirteen equally distant semitones or half-steps. All distinctions between major and minor tones and diatonic and chromatic semitones are swept away, and it is assumed that the sound between any two sounds in the scale is equally sharp and flat respectively to the sound immediately preceding and following it.

This method, of course, implies a rearrangement of the whole scale, for it is necessary to alter the precise pitch of every sound within the compass of the octave in order that the equalization may be effected. Thus it comes about that the equally tempered scale has only one interval tuned purely. This interval naturally is the octave. All the others require to be sharped or flatted in varying degrees. Every chord, every interval, with one exception, therefore, is more or less out of tune. The effect of this system of tempering cannot very well be noted accurately upon the pianoforte, owing to the evanescence of that instrument's tone; but the organ often shows the dissonance of certain intervals and chords in a most distressing manner. Perhaps the worst of the defects of the Equal Temperament are exhibited in the inability clearly to distinguish between true consonances and true dissonances. Where the actual distinctions between the true intervals are fused together it is impossible that there should be such distinctions between them as the true scale shows, and, consequently, we often are obliged to miss many delicate shades of comparative consonance or dissonance that would be clearly exhibited in a scale in which the intervals were represented with fidelity. We already know, however, that no such method is at present possible, and we must fain resign ourselves to the compromise that we have, and hope for better things in the future. But at the same time, the Equal Temperament possesses not a few positive virtues. As explained above, there can be no difference between the sharp of a given tempered sound and the flat of the tempered sound one whole step above the former. In other words, the sharp of C in the Equal Temperament must be the same as the flat of D, for these two sounds are assumed to be equally distant from the sound which is between them, and the three are simply part of a series of equal semitones. This being the case, the ambiguity that arises from the identity of these sounds is very often found to be invaluable for the purposes of quick and convenient modulation. There are instances in which the connecting link between two modulations would entirely be lost without the peculiar intonation that is afforded by equally tempered sounds. It seems, in short, that the equal temperament, imperfect and artificial as it is, cannot easily be replaced in the existing states of our acoustical knowledge and of the mechanical musical industries.

In order that the reader may more clearly realize the actual effects of the Equal Temperament upon musical intonation, the following table has been prepared, showing the differences of frequency between the true sounds of the just chromatic scale and the corresponding tempered sounds: (We are already familiar with the identity, in tempered intonation, of the sharps and flats of adjacent degrees of the scale.) C = 528 (Philharmonic Pitch).

True Scale.		Equally Tempered Scale.	
C	528	C	528
B	495	B	498 7/32
B flat	475 1/5	B flat—A sharp	470 7/20
A sharp	458 1/3	A	440
A	440	A flat—G sharp	417 1/20
A flat	422 2/5	G	391 11/20
G sharp	412 1/2	G flat—F sharp	373 7/20
G	396	F	342 4/10
G flat	380 4/25	E	332 17/20
F sharp	366 2/3	E flat—D sharp	313 19/20
F	352	D	296 7/20
E	330	D flat—C sharp	279 14/20
E flat	316 4/5	C	264
D sharp	309 11/24		
D	297		
D flat	285 3/25		
C sharp	275		
C	264		

It would be without the province of our immediate purpose to enter into any special discussion of the possibility of manufacturing pianofortes that shall give pure intonation, as distinguished from the tempered sounds that we have thus exhibited. We have already had occasion to mention that the Equal Temperament has become so strongly and intimately bound up with the performance of music, that the majority of musicians are probably incapable of distinguishing between the idea of pure as opposed to that of tempered musical sounds.

We have already pointed out, and reference to the various tables will confirm the assertion, that the Equal Temperament imposes excessive roughness of intonation upon very few of the musical intervals. Thus the octave is pure, the fourths and fifths nearly so, and only the seconds, thirds, sixths and sevenths are so rough as to be noticeable to other ears than those of the professional pianoforte tuner. Indeed it is very doubtful whether the musical public could ever be universally educated to the point of appreciating the differences between pure and equally-tempered fourths and fifths; while at the same time it must be remembered that the second and seventh, at least, are dissonances whether purely intoned or not.

We may properly question the actual advantage that the mechanical attainment of just pianoforte intonation would produce; we may ask ourselves what would be gained thereby for the cause of art, and the answer does not appear to be other than that any conceivable benefit must be so slight as to be practically negligible.

CHAPTER VII.
PIANOFORTE STRINGS AND THEIR PROPER DIMENSIONS.

The strings of a modern pianoforte are made of cast steel and possess a relatively great thickness and stiffness. That is to say, they enjoy these characteristics to a far greater degree than do the strings of any other musical instruments that employ such agents for the purpose of generating musical sounds. The strings of any member of the viol family, for example, are so totally unlike those of the pianoforte that no comparison of their respective behavior when subjected to tension can be of interest to any save the scientist. In dealing with the strings of the pianoforte then, we face an isolated and unusual problem which we shall have to consider at some length. We shall investigate the peculiar effects produced by the high tension, great thickness and great stiffness of the strings, as well as the singular phenomena exhibited in the case of the covered bass strings. We shall note that the strings are responsible for many unpleasant things of which they are seldom accused, and that their proportions as to length and tension do not comprehend in themselves the whole problem that the scaling of them presents to the designer. This matter of the internal nature of the steel and other wire has not, unhappily, received that attention to which its importance justly entitles it. No treatment of the principles of pianoforte design could be considered complete, however, without some discussion of the phenomena thus presented. The investigation which we shall undertake will lead us to the development of more of those general principles that we are now engaged in enunciating, and we shall then be able to formulate certain rules of wide application which may be employed in the practical consideration of the problems with which the whole matter of pianoforte design abounds.

As is generally known, the strings that are charged with the duty of emitting the sounds comprehended within the two lowest octaves on the pianoforte are customarily constructed of a combination of steel wire and some other, usually copper or iron. The latter is wound over a core of the former wire, and this winding is graduated, as to the amount and thickness of the material employed, according to the pitch to which it is desired that each string shall be tuned. There is an obvious reason for this procedure. For, as we have already shown, two strings whose lengths are as 2:1 will, other things being equal, emit musical sounds separated by the interval of an octave. Consequently, under perfect mechanical conditions, the length of each string of a pianoforte should conform to the rule thus indicated, and should be one-half or double the length of that which produces the octave above or below it; the absolute application of this rule, however, being subject to certain practical modifications throughout the entire compass. These will be discussed later.

Even in the absence of such considerations, however, this ideal condition could not be attained. The mechanical difficulties presented would always operate to forbid the carrying out of such an arrangement throughout the whole compass of the instrument. For, to follow the rule with entire consistency would necessitate a length of 256 inches for the lowest C, on an assumed length of 2 inches for the highest note of the same denomination. As this would imply a length or height of the instrument of nearly 24 feet it is not difficult to see that such construction is impossible. Furthermore, evenness of tone quality would be seriously hindered if the lowest strings were of any such dimensions. To secure equality of tonal result it is necessary, as has been noted above, that we should be able to equalize, as far as possible, the particular forms of vibration that pertain to each string. Obviously, the nature of the blow that would produce a given form of vibration in a string of 256 inches in length must be very different from that which would produce similar forms in a string only one-tenth as long. Again, to maintain such long strings at the required tension involves mechanical problems that savor more of engineering than of pianoforte building.

For these and cognate reasons, therefore, the practice has arisen of artificially slowing the rate of vibration in the bass strings by wrapping them with brass, iron or copper wire. Naturally, the form of the vibrations excited in these wrapped strings is entirely different from any that the plain steel wire is capable of producing. The iron or copper wire is itself thrown into vibration both independently of and together with the cord of steel, so that we have the phenomenon of one string emitting two separate series of vibrations, with resultant disarrangement of the generated upper partials and concomitant production of beats in a more or less appreciable quantity. Now if, in addition, the bass strings are not scaled with approximate correctness as to their relative lengths, thicknesses, and other dimensions, it follows that there will be two distinct and different causes of dissonance and unevenness of tone-quality, either of which is sufficient, in itself, to produce very unpleasant tonal results. It is clear, then, that particular attention must be paid to the designing of the string arrangement, if excellence of tone-quality is to be anywhere approached.

It is, fortunately, possible to give quite precise directions for the calculating of string dimensions. As a preliminary, we must remind the reader of the rules that were laid down in Chapter IV, relating to the behavior of stretched strings. It will be recalled that we had occasion to observe that these rules would require certain modifications in practice, as they referred only to ideal musical strings which are of perfect flexibility and perfect uniformity, and are stretched at an absolutely constant tension.

The first modification that appears upon investigation has reference to the division of string-lengths. It has already been pointed out that, in practice, we cannot obtain the octave above the fundamental tone of a given pianoforte string by dividing it exactly in the middle. Conversely, an exact doubling of the length does not produce the exact octave below the given fundamental tone. This discrepancy occurs on account of the fact that the shortening or lengthening of a given string causes a corresponding change in the tension at which it is maintained and in the density of adhesion of its molecules.

Now if we double the length of a string in order to obtain the octave below its fundamental tone, we decrease its tension, and this causes a slowing of the frequency of vibration. Then again, the increased resiliency of the string brought about by the lengthening tends also to decrease the frequency. The frequencies of vibration of a string vary directly as the square root of the tension, inversely as the thickness, and directly also as the stiffness. These axioms being admitted, we observe that to obtain an octave lower than a given fundamental tone, we must obtain one-half the frequency that produces the fundamental. Therefore, as we see from above, the double length must be decreased by one-fourth to allow for the automatic decrease of stiffness which varies directly as the frequency. And this modification must itself be modified to compensate for the increase in frequency produced by the very act of shortening. Therefore we must consider the tension, and we find that to reduce this tends again to decrease the stiffness in exactly the same proportions as it was before increased. But frequency of vibration varies as the square root of the tension; therefore we take the square root of one-fourth, which was the fraction first arrived at. This root is one-sixteenth and is the differential factor that must be subtracted from the ideal octave lengths, in order to obtain the practical lengths.

It will be found of course, as must be apparent to the reader, that the differential factor here suggested does not provide a complete solution to the problem of allowing for the exhibited differences between theory and practice. It does, however, provide a true guide to the lengths. There is of course a difference of produced frequency to be allowed for yet. Fortunately, however, this is provided for by the graduated thicknesses of pianoforte wire. By taking advantage of this almost geometrically proportioned graduation of diameter we are able to calculate a stringing scale that, if adhered to, will give the nearest possible approximation to complete harmony between theory and practice. That is to say, we can proceed with a string-length calculation based upon the differential factor already obtained, and then by arranging the distribution of the string thicknesses according to the diameters that are provided by the manufacturers of music wire, we may obtain a true estimation, not only as to the thickness of wire to be used at each place, but also as to the lengths proper to each string. Of course the reader will remember that the matter of pitch is of considerable importance in all calculations of this kind. A difference in pitch implies difference of tension when the other factors remain equal, and we therefore have calculated the following tables on the assumption that the pitch to be used is that known as the International or C 517. Attention is, therefore, directed to the following

TABLE SHOWING TRUE LENGTHS OF OCTAVE STRINGS FROM THE HIGHEST C STRING TO THE LAST C STRING THAT IS USUALLY LEFT UNWRAPPED.

C^5		= 2.048 in.	= 2 1/25	+ ... Approx.
C^4	= 2.048 × 1.9375	= 3.968 in.	= 3 24/25	+ ... "
C^3	= 3.968 × 1.9375	= 7.688 in.	= 7 17/25	+ ... "
C^2	= 7.688 × 1.9375	= 14.875 in.	= 14 7/8	+ ... "
C^1	= 14.875 × 1.9375	= 28.820 in.	= 28 4/5	+ ... "
C	= 28.820 × 1.9375	= 55.828 in.	= 55 4/5	+ ... "

[NOTE.—The length of the first string is chosen arbitrarily, but as given is a very close approximation to the practice of the best American makers. The vulgar fractions are calculated from the decimals and the error in no case exceed about one-fiftieth of an inch. The differential factor is, as we know, 1/16. Therefore we multiply by (2 − 1/16) or 1 15/16; in decimals 1.9375.]

The above table, then, affords us a reliable guide to the scaling of the unwrapped strings. At the same time, however, it is not by any means complete, for the reason that there is no method shown as yet for the calculation of the other and intermediate string-lengths. We are, however, able to accomplish this task by the aid of a very ingenious rule proposed by the late Professor Pole, F.R.S. It is as follows:

The proper length of any string may be determined from that of any other string, provided that the length and frequency of the second string be known. Given these factors: Then,

1.   Take the logarithm of the length of the known string.

2.   Multiply the number .025086 by the number of semitones that the sound to be given by the required string length is above or below the sound produced by the given string.

3.   If the required string is below the given string, add together the two numbers obtained; if it be above, subtract the second number from the first; the result in both cases is the logarithm of the required length.

For example, we have calculated already the proper length of C. In hundredths of an inch this length is expressed as 2882. The log. of this number is 45943. (This may be verified by any table of logarithms.)

It is required to obtain the length of the string that, *caeteris paribus*, will produce one semitone above C.

	45943	= log. of 2882
	02508 (6)	= .02508 (6) × the number (1) of semitones that required string sounds above given string
By subtraction,	43435	= log. of 2718 = length of required string in hundredths of an inch

∴ Required length for C-sharp = 27 $\frac{18}{100}$ inches

By reversing the process described above, and adding instead of subtracting, the proper lengths for the semitone below and all others in descending progression may be calculated with accuracy.

Having thus settled the matter of string lengths, we may proceed to consider the questions of diameter. But it is first of all necessary to warn the reader that the lengths that have here been calculated refer only to such pianofortes as are capable, by reason of their size, of taking the ideal string-lengths. Very small uprights, for example, cannot be brought within that classification, except as regards the highest of their strings. In all pianofortes, no matter what their size, the higher strings are practically identical in length; but it will be found that shortness of height in an upright or of length in a grand begins, towards the middle of the scale, disastrously to affect the string proportions. As already pointed out, there are only two ways in which these disproportions can be overcome. These are through alterations in the tension or in the thickness. But such alterations necessarily disturb the whole tonal balance; and here we find a very strong reason for the poor tone that the average atrophied grand or upright possesses. Moreover, it must not be forgotten that disproportionate thickness or unduly slackened tension affect the actual nature of the vibrations that are set up within the string. And the affections are operative both as to frequency and to form. Therefore, naturally, bad tone and inability to stand in tune. This is not intended as an argument against the small pianoforte; but it is desired here to show that these little instruments, whether horizontal or vertical, must not be expected to perform impossibilities. If we are obliged to build small instruments, we must revise our calculations and tabulate the string-lengths according to a different basis of apportionment. For the purpose of the present work, however, the calculations have been made on the assumption that the standard size of pianoforte is to be designed.

Turn we then to the consideration of string diameters. The cast steel wire that is used for the pianoforte strings is supplied in definitely numbered and graded thicknesses. The numbers that are used generally run from No. 13 to No. 24. According to the tests made at the Chicago World's Fair by the aid of Riehle Bros.' testing machine, the wire of these numbers was of the following diameters and broke at the following strains. The wire manufactured by the firm of Moritz Poehlmann, Nuremberg, Germany, has been selected from among the various products that were subjected to these tests, on account of its superior durability and evenness of gradation.

Number	Diameter in fractions of an inch	Broke at strain of
13	.030	325 lbs.
14	.031	335 lbs.
15	.032	350 lbs.
16	.035	400 lbs.
17	.037	415 lbs.
18	.040	
19	.042	
20	.044	

Now it is a well known fact, and, indeed, obvious from what has already been said, that the proportional relations as to length, tension, diameter and breaking strain do not permit any other arrangement for the scaling of wire than that which is universally accepted by piano makers. That is to say, the shortest wires are taken from the thinnest numbers, and vice-versa, the whole scaling being so arranged as to secure for each tone that its strings shall be stretched at approximately the same tension. Experience and the observations of the most eminent manufacturers seem to have established that the strain upon each of the uncovered strings should be maintained, as nearly as possible, at 160 lbs. If this be done it will be found that a pianoforte so constructed will produce the proper pitch at each string when the lengths are as calculated in the tables referred to. It will, of course, be necessary to arrange with due proportion the number of strings that are to be taken from the wire of each number. It will be found that the best practice takes into account the half sizes not shown here and strings the instrument with an average of five tones to each thickness of wire, beginning at 13 or 13 ½ and continuing down to the end of the unwrapped strings according to the general directions suggested. Experience and the individual ideas of the designer, assisted by such knowledge as this work aims to impart, are the best guides that can be followed. Empirical induction, based upon observation and experience, provides the only possible and practical means for arriving at the true and proper arrangements to be made for each individual instrument. This empiricism extends with particular force to all string arrangements and is seen nowhere so conspicuously as in the variety of methods that are adopted by manufacturers in determining the number of strings within the unwrapped sections of the scale. Thus, certain makers carry the wrapping over to the beginning of the treble strings and have two or three string-groups provided with wrapped wire before the overstringing is begun. The idea here is either to correct original defects of scale design or to shade down the break in tone that so often occurs at the point where the overstringing usually begins. From observation of the practice of the best makers, it may be said that the tone C below middle C is usually the first overstrung tone. Of course, when the instrument is very small it will often be found that it is impossible to give the last unwrapped strings their proper lengths. In this case these offending strings may either be covered with light wrapping or may be put bodily over into the overstrung portion of the scale, in which latter case they will be wrapped anyway.

Supposing then that the matter of the number of overstrung strings has been determined, we may proceed to the consideration of the dimensions, number and covering of the strings that are to serve here. We are obliged to confess that the problem of attaining to good tone in the bass is, indeed, difficult. It is by no means hopeless, however, as the success of more than one eminent maker has already demonstrated.

The simplest, most obvious, and easiest way out of the inherent difficulties of the scaling of bass strings is to be found in the consideration of their proper lengths. It does not require very much thought to perceive the truth that the longer the strings the less weight need be imposed upon them. If, in fact, we make the bass strings to approach as far as may be to the lengths that they would require to have if unwrapped, we shall be able to reduce proportionally the amount of artificial control that has to be exercised over the vibration speed. Not only this, but the greater length thus attained implies greater tension. That is to say that, as we saw before, the tension at which a string is stretched acts to overcome the slowness of vibration-speed induced by its greater length, and, consequently, tends to generate a more regular progression of the upper partials (as experiment has demonstrated), with resultant tendency to greater purity of tone-quality.

We may, in fact, accept it as an axiom that the bass strings should be as long and, simultaneously, as lightly weighted as possible, and that the weight of them should be strictly proportioned to the pitch of the musical tone that they are desired, at a given tension, to emit. As far as the second clause of these conditions is concerned it is well to remind the reader that limitations of space within the body of a piano usually determine the possible lengths of the bass strings. So much so is this the case, indeed, that it is not often possible to make any great difference in their respective lengths. The best makers appear to be agreed in a method of treating the problem that is at once simple and effective. They recognize the great advantage of scaling the bass strings at the greatest possible length, and then they take care that the descending increase of length is no greater than to make the lowest bass string one-fifth longer than the highest. At the same time they so graduate the weight of the wrapping material that the same results are attained as would naturally follow if they were as accurately scaled, in proportionate length, as are the plain wire strings.

This equalization is, of course, only approximate. For the forms of vibration excited in two strings of the same pitch will be different whenever the various factors that govern the emission of sound by them are variable. Thus when the factor of length is varied, no counter-adjustment of tension, thickness or density can restore to the string so modified the exact form of vibration that it may have originally possessed. Consequently it becomes impossible to induce from artificially weighted strings precisely the same series of partial tones that a plain wire filament will emit, even when the tones generated by the two strings are of the same pitch.

The lesson of this is plain. As perfection of tonal quality can only be attained in part, it especially behooves us to pay strict attention to such scaling of the bass strings as will furnish a complement of sound producing agencies that may be relied upon to induce as nearly as possible the same successions of partials as are habitually emitted throughout the higher sections of the piano. Thus it becomes evident that the greatest practicable length and the least practicable weight are the chief factors that must govern the designer in laying out the scale for the bass strings.

The relative densities of the wrapping material employed in the manufacture of bass strings have been the subject of considerable study. Brass, which was the earliest object of experiment, has long been superseded by either copper or iron. As to the relative advantages possessed by these two materials, it can be said at once that the chief and almost the only advantage presented by the latter lies in its relative cheapness. Acoustically, however, copper forms by all means the most suitable material for the winding of bass strings, and this for the following reasons: The specific gravity of copper is 8.78, while that of iron is but 7.78. Again, the former metal, while inferior in tenacity to the latter, possesses, on the other hand, the great advantage of higher ductility, so that its elastic qualities are very marked. It is thus evident that copper is a more suitable material for the generation of musical sound than is iron, and the qualities which we have just noted as pertaining to it are precisely those most useful in the production of harmonic progressions of partial tones. It is therefore clear that as between copper and iron all the advantages lie with the former.

The thickest wire used for the uncovered strings is generally No. 24. In beginning the scaling of the bass strings, however, we choose No. 17 or No. 18 for the notes nearest to the treble. The covering is usually from No. 25 to No. 28 (standard, not music, wire gauge) according to the size of the piano and the practicable string-length. Of course, longer strings may be covered with lighter wire. The first covered string is generally approximately one-sixth shorter than the string immediately above it. This proportion, as suggested above, may, however, be profitably disregarded, if it thereby be possible to lengthen the bass strings. There are always two of these strings to each tone and the thickness of covering wire must be progressively increased as the scale descends. A descending increase of one number in thickness of the covering wire for each pair of strings may properly be allowed, unless the lengths are too closely alike, or vice-versa, in which cases suitable modifications may be made. But assuming that the descending lengths are arranged in arithmetical progression with a mean of ¾ of an inch, and supposing the highest covered string to be 45 inches long; then the suggested increase of thickness should under all circumstances hold good. It may often be found, however, that the space limitations of an instrument or other practical considerations make it impossible to follow out these rules with exactitude. In any case, we must remember that all such rules are themselves the fruit of empirical observation and to such observations we must look, when it becomes necessary to revise them in order to satisfy the requirements of some particular situation.

CHAPTER VIII.
RESONANCE AND THE RESONANCE-APPARATUS OF THE PIANOFORTE.

We have now made a somewhat lengthy and thorough investigation into the nature and behavior of the various materials and substances that are employed in the construction of pianoforte strings. From this inquiry we have been able to deduce a set of rules which, when practically applied, will furnish us with a guide to the solution of many perplexing problems which take their root in the conditions imposed upon the designer by the limitations of space and the other mechanical conditions of pianoforte construction. It would not be proper, however, to proceed forthwith to the practical questions of support for the strings. For we must still find the correct solutions of another series of problems that spring, not from the strings themselves, but from their important and necessary accessories, the sound-board and belly bridges.

The belly-bridge is the medium of connection between the strings and the sound-board. Through it the vibrations excited in the strings are conveyed to the freely vibrating surface of the sound-board, and the sonority of the generated sounds is thereby enormously increased. This is the process in bare outline, but, in order to obtain a proper view of the matter under discussion it will be necessary to examine the phenomena to which the juxtaposition of strings, bridge and sound-board give rise. We must, in fact, make another brief excursion into the realms of acoustics.

The property which the sound-board possesses of reinforcing and emphasizing the sounds generated by the strings is called "resonance." Important as this property of sonorous bodies is to musicians and the makers of musical instruments, the fact remains that it is a matter very little understood by the mass of them. This is the more remarkable when one considers that, without resonant properties, no musical instruments would be possible. For it is not difficult to perceive that music, as we know it, could not exist were the means of expressing it limited to the actual and immediate bodies that perform the motions which are the direct causes of musical sounds. This fact is most clearly illustrated in the case of the pianoforte. The unaided sound of a pianoforte string is ridiculously feeble; in fact, it is quite inaudible at the distance of a few feet. Yet we are all familiar with the wonderfully harmonious and powerful sounds that the same string will be the means of producing when aided by the sound-board.

Resonance may be defined as the property which one sonorous body possesses of impressing its vibrations upon another sonorous body. The existence of this power may be demonstrated in a variety of ways. The most simple proofs are afforded by the pianoforte itself. For example, if we strike any key upon the instrument and at the same time gently press down the corresponding key one octave higher, so as to raise the damper without at the same time raising the hammer, we shall find that if the first key be released while the other is held open, the string corresponding to the latter will continue to give its proper sound. In this case the vibrations excited in the first string travel along the belly-bridge until they reach the nearest open string whose vibration rate is synchronous with that of the original sounding string. When such a string is reached it is immediately impressed with the motions excited in the former string, with the results above described. This is a case of resonance of two attached bodies. Peculiar as it may seem, however, it is not *essential* as a preliminary condition to the existence of resonance between them that two sonorous bodies be tangibly connected. For instance, the foregoing experiment may be varied by employing two pianofortes and choosing one of the sounds from each. The result will be precisely the same. It will, however, be noted that only such sounds as have either synchronous or nearly synchronous rates of vibration will exhibit the phenomena of resonance when separated from each other. Where they are connected, however, especially when the connecting body is a sound-board prepared for the purpose, synchronism is not necessary. In fact, it is a matter of common observation that the sound-board of the pianoforte, in conjunction with the belly-bridge, operates to set up more or less intense vibration in every string within the compass of the instrument when the dampers are raised, even if only one string be struck. When the damper pedal is raised in playing, every string throughout the instrument is immediately thrown into a state of vibration, and begins to sound. The result is a large augmentation of the total volume of sound produced. Of course, the sound of any one string thus sympathetically excited is relatively feeble, but the total volume is considerable, with especial strength in the particular partials of each string that are more or less synchronous, as to their vibration rates, with the sounds originally produced by striking the keys. When the dampers are permitted to rest in their normal positions, on the other hand, the sound-board exercises its resonant powers in a different manner. Whenever a string or group of strings are struck, the board is thrown into a state of vibration which affects only itself and not the strings that remain damped. The result of this excitement is to expose a relatively great vibrating surface to the atmosphere, with the immediate consequence that the quantity of air impelled into a state of periodic motion is multiplied many times. Thus the size of the impelled layers of air, and the resultant sonorous waves is augmented until we obtain sounds of the intensity and richness which we are accustomed to associate with the pianoforte.

Now, from what we have already learned of the laws of tone-quality, it is obvious that the resonant medium must be capable of reinforcing not only the fundamental but the partials of all the tones which it influences. To this end we must provide a substance that combines elasticity with the freedom of vibration that is, of course, essential. It is not possible to employ metal on account of its excessive stiffness and consequent resistance to the influence of impressed vibrations; while on the other hand a wooden body will not be sufficiently stiff and rigid unless artificially strengthened. For this reason it is customary to construct sound-boards of a freely-vibrating wood (the spruce-fir is generally employed for this purpose) and to strengthen them by fastening to one side bars of hard wood called "ribs." In this manner the requisite stiffness is imparted to the board, which at the same time is sufficiently susceptible to the impressed vibrations from the strings.

It is a fact that this accepted and universal form of resonance table is essentially similar to that which was used in the ancient harpsichord and spinet. While there has been much experimentation along these lines, it does not appear that any lasting improvements have been devised as yet, at least in the governing principles of sound-board construction. We may then confine ourselves to a description of the accepted styles.

The wood used in the construction of sound-boards is the spruce-fir, which, as stated above, has been found to be the best possible for the purpose. It is prepared in a sheet of suitable size, and is arranged so that the grain runs approximately at right angles to the plane of the belly-bridge.

It can easily be understood that the thickness of the board must vary according to the dimensions of the strings that act upon it. In other words, we can perceive that more resonating power is required for the relatively weaker treble strings than for the relatively stronger bass strings. The actual thicknesses vary with individual makers. From $\frac{3}{8}$ inch in the treble to $\frac{1}{4}$ of an inch in the bass may be regarded as a fair approximation. Nevertheless, it is necessary to bear in mind that these dimensions are subject to modification according to the variations in the total amount of tension that the instrument is made to bear. Other things being equal, an increased tension load implies a thicker board, and vice-versa.

After the dimensions and material of the board are thus determined, it remains to consider the bridging, the reinforcement, and the adjustment of the board. We shall consider these in their natural order, as given above.

The belly-bridges are placed upon the surface of the board, as we know, for the purpose of conveying to the latter the minute blows that are inflicted by the vibrating strings, in order that the vibrations may be impressed upon the board and there amplified and intensified as described at the beginning of this chapter. A secondary duty is that of delimiting the lower boundaries of the speaking length of the strings. The bridges must naturally be constructed with a curved outline that is determined during the draughting of the scale.

The actual shape of this curve has no effect *per se*, upon the activities of the bridge, but has to do entirely with the string lengths. The bridge which carries the overstrung portion of the scale may be considered as being similarly affected, as to outline, by the exigencies of the bass string dimensions. The bridges are made of hard wood, and their sizes are usually from one inch and one-quarter to one inch and one-half high, and in width about one-eighth of an inch less all round. The variations occur principally on account of the necessity which arises of giving a bearing to the strings as they cross over the bridges.

It is necessary that the strings be raised at the bridges in order that they may be firmly held at the points of contact by means of the strain imposed by them on the surface of the bridge when they are stretched at proper tension. Of course it is most essential that this bearing be not too high, as in that case the strain becomes too much for the board to bear with facility and its durability is thereby impaired. The necessary immobility of the portions of the strings that lie upon the bridge is secured by diverting the line of travel, and causing them to bear against pins placed on either edge of the bridge, so as to slant the line of the string as it passes over. The waste ends should run parallel to the speaking-length after the bridge has been crossed.

It may be further properly remarked that there are interesting and complicated problems to be overcome in choosing the material and the exact method of building the belly-bridges. It is desired to combine extreme facility of vibration with the requisite resisting power. In other words, the bridge must allow the fullest possible scope to the impressed vibrations from the strings and, at the same time, must possess such strength that it can successfully resist the torsions imposed upon it by the pull of the strings. The only method that appears to be thoroughly practical and, at the same time, acoustically correct is one which most manufacturers have already had the acuteness to adopt. The bridge, according to this method, is built up of a number of layers of hard wood (generally maple) which are glued together in such a way that the grain of each layer crosses that of the other. In this way both the requisite strength and more or less facility of vibration are obtained. But it has remained for one distinguished piano maker to go a step further, and to apply thoroughly scientific methods to the design of the belly-bridges. In the instruments made by him, he has built the bridges in such a way that the impressed vibrations will travel *in the line of* the grain instead of across it. The bridges, in fact, are built of end-grain and not, as is general, of cross-grain wood. This ingenious and simple device facilitates the passage of the impressed vibrations and, in consequence, tends to impart a greater clarity to the various partials of the compound tones. Some existing pianofortes might be greatly improved as to their clarity of speech if a similar device for increasing the power of resonance were fitted to them.

There is another point to be emphasized in reference to the bridges. In some makes of pianos the line of the bridge construction is permitted to be broken wherever there is a corresponding break in the hammer line caused by the interposition of the various braces of the iron frame. The obvious result of such a method of construction is that the resonance of the board is much interfered with and the consequent tonal efficiency of the instrument lessened. For it is easy to see that if the bridge line be broken at any point, the vibrations that are carried from any sounding string along the bridge to the surface of the sound-board will be stopped at the break and will be unable to reach those parts of the board that are remote from its path, with rapidity and ease. Incontestably, therefore, the bridge line should, if possible, be continuous. Many manufacturers, however, while apparently recognizing the force of this proposition, seem to be afraid to follow it out to its logical conclusion. They are willing to make the line of bridge continuous until the end of the plain wire strings is reached. After that point they seem to think that it is no longer necessary that continuity of communication between the various sounding members of the scale should subsist. This idea is, of course, quite fallacious. The bass strings are simply a continuation of the higher ones, and are, in fact, precisely similar except in regard to the details of thickness and length. Moreover, it is quite as important that the portions of the board over which the bass bridge exercises control should be made freely resonant, as it is that this process should be applied to the others. The bass bridge ought invariably, therefore, to be connected with the bridges that serve the rest of the strings.

The reinforcement of the board is accomplished by gluing ribs of wood across its back surface in a direction crossing the grain of the board. These ribs are usually made about one inch square in the middle portions. This size is continued until near the edge of the board on each side, when they are gradually pared down in a graceful curve until at the actual edge the thickness is no more than about one-thirty-second of an inch. According to the most approved modern practice it is found advisable to pocket these ribs into the wooden framing of the instrument, by continuing them past the edge of the sound board and making suitable apertures in the framing, into which the extensions are adjusted and fastened. This has the effect of holding the board more firmly in its fastenings and also of preventing the early loosening of the ribs from their places; an occurrence which causes much rattling, and complete impairment of tonal quality. It is usual to have twelve ribs upon the surface of the board, but the number may be varied whenever it is considered necessary. If it is required to give specially ample support to the board on account of unusually great strain, or for any other reason, the number may be increased, but such procedure must be taken with caution, as too many ribs weight the board to such an extent as to deaden its power of molecular and undulatory vibration. This must at all costs be avoided.

It is usual to glue the ribs upon the surface of the board first—that is before the bridges—and good practice dictates that the surface of the board be dried out in a hot-box for at least 24 hours before either of these processes take place. If this be carried out properly, the resultant shrinking of the wood will be taken up after the board has become thoroughly cooled, and if the process is repeated when the board is glued into the framing of the instrument, the result will be to endow it with a natural "crown," or arch, caused by the reactive swelling that takes place after the artificially induced shrinking.

Although the above methods of ribbing are to be considered the best and as representing the most advanced practice, yet it will be found that some makers dispose the ribs in a fan-like manner, having the diverging points of the fan at the upper end of the board, while others adopt an oblique disposition and arrange them as before described. Also, we find a straight up-and-down arrangement whereby the ribs are glued parallel to the plane of the treble strings. We term these three styles the fan form, the oblique form, and the vertical form respectively.

As for the comparative advantages of the three types of construction thus described, it may be said that they all represent individual features that are more or less beneficial. For example, the fan-like disposition gives a greater number of long ribs, while the oblique form provides more of separate units. The vertical system may be considered as a mean between the other two.

In general, we shall be well advised in remembering that the prime function of ribbing is to increase the tension of the board and its elasticity, and thus to promote the power of resonance. A secondary function is that of providing extra resisting power. Now it is obvious that both of these duties can be better performed by a multiplicity of ribs, and consequently a system is to be recommended that permits the employment of the largest total area of ribbing. At the same time unduly long ribs are not good, for they have a greater tendency to become loose and to spring up from the surface of the board, with dire results to tone and durability. It would therefore seem that the oblique disposition has more to recommend it than the others, since it provides enough total ribbing area without imposing inconveniently long ribbing units upon the surface of the board.

When the ribbing of the sound-board and the fixing of the bridges has been accomplished, it remains to adjust the completed structure within the wooden back-framing of the instrument. It is necessary that the board be so secured that it shall acquire a position analogous to that of a stretched membrane—at least as far as concerns the rigidity with which its edges are fixed to the framing. There are several methods for obtaining the required rigidity of the edges of the board. The natural or artificial crowning of the board's surface is best attained through the medium of particularly rigid edge fastening; and the adoption of a continuous closing rim for the board, as in certain grand pianofortes, together with the use of a system of screw compression, alike indicate the various directions in which the ideas of experimenters have led them. The underlying notion in all these devices is to endow the vibrating surface with both elasticity and durability to an extent that could not be attained with the unaided wood.

The gluing of the sound-board to the framing is a process that demands the greatest skill and care. It is essential that the board be warmed, and that the glue which is used be in just the proper condition; neither too thick nor too thin, and, above all, boiling hot. If the fastening be done when the board is in the shrunken condition described above, and with the required skill and care, it will be found that the fibres of the wood have been squeezed together so as to raise the center part of the board somewhat above the level of the edges. This gives what we have denominated the "crown," and is important as affecting the durability and resisting power of the entire board. It must be remembered that by relieving the sound-board of as much as possible of the strain imposed by the strings, we are able to increase its durability and to preserve its tone-producing quality more surely than is otherwise possible. Boards that are not so protected must inevitably become entirely flattened out in the course of a few years. When this happens the level of the belly-bridge sinks and the bearing of the strings upon the latter is destroyed. Hence an immediate and inevitable deterioration of tone quality. For the altering of the level in this manner affects the impression of the vibrations of the strings upon the bridges and hence upon the board itself. If the height of the bridges be too great, the bearing of the strings upon them will likewise be excessive, and the board will be crushed down in the same manner. If, however, the directions as to bridging, ribbing and adjustment that have been given are followed with discretion, the troubles outlined here are likely at least to be minimized.

Of course, the later care of the pianoforte after it is sold has much to do with the manifold troubles that occur within the entire resonance apparatus. These things cannot be foreseen, and it is, therefore, most essential to guard against them as much as possible by careful attention to the details of construction and adjustment.

Lastly, we may observe that the practice of screwing the bridges down on to the board by screws driven in from the rear is to be condemned. While it is undoubtedly advantageous to take some measure to increase the permanency of the fastening, it will be found that it is far better, acoustically, to provide the bridge with wooden dowels and glue these into suitable holes in the board. Thus the conducting power of the bridge is increased and the vibrating surface of the sound-board is not broken up by the insertion of foreign metallic substances. Another and concomitant advantage is the absence of the wooden washers under the heads of these bridge-screws. Such devices are too often, as they become loose, a source of rattling and jingling.

It is well to be rid of them, as of all possible things that are likely to be similarly affected by wear or atmospheric conditions.

CHAPTER IX.
THE CASE AND FRAMING OF THE PIANOFORTE.

The grand pianoforte is distinguished conspicuously from the upright, as far as concerns the principles of its construction, by the different function which its exterior casing exercises. As was stated in Chapter III, the exterior walls of the upright have no part in the bearing or resisting work that the iron and wooden framing performs. They exist chiefly for the purpose of giving support to the key-board and action, and of affording a foundation whereon may be constructed the elaborate architectural and decorative structure that, in its entirety, is denominated the pianoforte case.

The synonymous portions of the grand pianoforte, on the contrary, have a far more important duty to fulfill. While they are equally charged with the support of the key-frame and action, they are also an essential part of the wooden framing, are one and homogeneous with it, and, in fact, occupy much the same position as what is known as the "back" of the upright, as well as being the external and decorative coverings of the instrument.

The case of the grand is constructed of a series of continuous veneers, glued one upon another, and each extending completely around the periphery of the case. These veneers are glued at cross grain to prevent splitting and are applied to the pianoforte and bent into shape when in a heated state. The complete outline thus obtained is denominated the "continuous bent rim" and is a distinguishing feature of the modern grand pianoforte as made in America. Several eminent German makers, as Bechstein, also employ similar means of constructing the external walls. In England, on the contrary, the case is usually made out of one thickness of wood bent into the required shape by steam and joined in several places. This system provides for separate moldings for the bent and straight sides and for the rear portion.

The advantage claimed for the continuous bent rim is that the whole case, by this means, becomes so closely bound up with the rest of the structure as to become part of one homogeneous resonant whole, thus improving the general resonance and imparting a *sostenuto* and *cantabile* that can in no other manner be attained.

While data are lacking for the precise investigation of this claim, it is significant that the bent rim method has not only become universal among American makers—by one of them it was first devised—but has even made its way into European favor.

The case, after it has been bent in this manner into the proper shape, has to be decoratively veneered according to the style of ornamentation that is intended for it. The work of veneering these cases, whether for uprights or grands, need not be gone into here in detail. There are so many specialists in this department who confine themselves to the turning out of such veneered cases, and the whole matter is so far away from the principles of pianoforte construction, that it is not considered necessary to go into it here.

It is, of course, required to provide the case of the grand pianoforte with a system of wooden struts which bind it together and give it strength and resisting power. These struts are set into the case in the general form of the letter A, having the apex at the forward end of the case. At this apex they are crossed by another wooden strut running parallel to the key-board, which serves to bind them together and to mark the limit of the space to be occupied by the sound-board. These struts are not, as we may thus see, carried into the very front of the case, but are confined to that portion which is directly underneath the sound-board. In front of this space is left the gap through which the action is later to strike, and underneath is provided a key-bed to carry the action and keys. The key-bed joins the front portions of the bent rim and closes the casing in the front, thus providing a definite and uniform structure. Above the key-bed and in front of the gap is one of the most important parts of the entire instrument. It is called the "wrest-plank," and is situated at the foremost portion of the case. This wrest-plank is built of a series of hard wooden layers, glued together at cross grain and adapted to be bored with holes in which are placed the "wrest-pins," or tuning-pins, that control the tension of the strings. This block or plank must necessarily be of great solidity and be capable of holding the pins frictionally, so that they will not pull round under the immense strains that are imposed upon them.

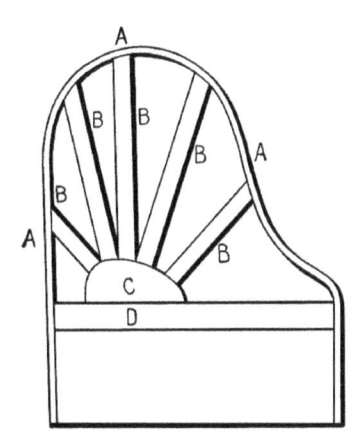

MODERN METHOD OF GRAND PIANOFORTE CASE CONSTRUCTION.

- **A. Continuous bent rim.**
- **B. Wooden struts.**
- **C. Iron shoe holding struts and connecting with iron plate.**
- **D. Main beam.**

The gap which is necessary in the grand pianoforte between the sound-board and the tuning-pins makes it impossible to join the former to the wrest-plank. This state of affairs undoubtedly constitutes a weakness inherent in the grand and, besides, exceedingly unfortunate. For an interruption of the continuity of communication between the various sound-conducting materials of which the instrument is constructed entails a corresponding loss of resonance. The tone of the pianoforte is inevitably fleeting and evanescent; lack of continuity in the construction only increases this fault. It has somewhere been stated that the construction of the grand pianoforte implies greater resisting strength of the wrest-plank on account of its being entirely supported by the iron frame and not dependent upon a wooden back as in the upright. This view seems to be incorrect. A properly supported back on an upright affords a very strong support to the wrest-plank and in combination with the iron frame supplies all necessary rigidity, and in a manner more direct and efficient. But the wrest-plank of the grand pianoforte may and should possess a sufficient strength. Various makers have adopted several different methods to secure this strength. One very good device supplies a rear truss to the lower surface of the wrest-plank by means of a downward projecting shoulder cast in the iron frame. There are other methods more or less similar. The arrangement of the tuning-pins within the body of the wrest-plank also requires considerable care. Of course, their disposition depends ultimately upon the string arrangement, but there are problems to be considered in connection with the manner in which they are arranged with relation to their mutual positions as considered apart from the strings. For example, it is most important that they should be so placed that the strings do no rub against each other in their passage between the pins and the agraffes. The frequent neglect of this matter is a cause for regret. Much loss of tonal purity would be avoided and the tuner's work greatly simplified if all designers took the proper amount of care in this important matter. Further, it may be remarked that the best practice accords with this suggestion in every respect. It will also be found that a slight tilting back of the pins in a direction that is remote from the strings tends to lighten the pull of the latter and to assist the resisting power of the wrest-plank.

When the iron plate is fastened over the entire structure, it is fixed on to the wrest-plank by means of heavy iron bolts that should be sufficiently long to go entirely through it and be closed with a nut on the other side. By this means the wrest-plank is secured against lack of rigidity, and its durability immensely increased.

The hardest kind of maple should be used in the construction of the wrest-plank. No other wood appears to have so many of the required qualities, and its use for this purpose has become, in America at least, universal.

The general details of the external case of the grand pianoforte are not unfamiliar. The standard full size of nine feet and the miniature of six feet or less, as well as intermediate parlor sizes, are familiar to all. The shape of the fall-board that covers the keys is well known, and the design of the lid and supporting legs sufficiently common to make further description superfluous. It is proper, however, to note briefly the general change that has come about in the conception of the decorative function of the grand pianoforte case.

Formerly, the aim of pianoforte manufacturers was entirely different from that of the early harpsichord and spinet makers. Instead of doing their utmost to improve the external æsthetic value of their instruments, they seemed too much occupied in providing means for internal improvement to pay proper attention to appearance. Thus we see that the sombre and hideous decorative ideas which prevailed in the furniture of the last generation were long faithfully imitated in the external design of the grand pianoforte. The ugly and cumbersome carved legs, the inartistic curving of the lid and arms, and the general look of ponderosity and hugeness all combined to give to the instrument of that era the general appearance of a hypertrophied coffin on legs.

Modern makers, however, animated by a truer appreciation of decorative values, and recognizing the refining influence of beautiful things, in themselves, and apart from their other properties, have gone far towards consigning the more crude and hideous designs to the limbo of obscurity. It has become generally recognized that the coffin-like look of the concert grand may be largely modified, if not wholly removed. By altering the design of the legs and by regarding them rather as a part of the case than as mere supports, it has been possible to combine the proportions of legs and case so as to make them appear one harmonious entity. Of course, the actual method of attaining to this end has varied largely among different makers, and, likewise, the greater number of successful efforts in the direction suggested have been made upon grand pianofortes designed to order to fit the furnishings and decorative schemes of music rooms in the homes of the wealthy. Nevertheless it is a healthy sign of the general æsthetic development of the American people that the number of these specially ordered and designed cases increases yearly. In this way we are going back to the ideals that possessed the ancient makers of the virginals, clavichords and other instruments, who were wont to call in the services of the most famous artists in color and the most cunning carvers in wood to compass their beautiful and costly designs.

It is true that the stock styles of grand pianoforte cases are usually plain as to contour and decoration, but no one now can deny to them grace and purity of outline or beauty and richness of material. On the other hand, the practice increases yearly of keeping in stock cases made in such styles as the Chippendale, the Sheraton and the Empire, to say nothing of the perennial and truly American Colonial designs. The fact that these numerous varieties all find purchasers is a striking commentary on the growing taste and refinement of the general public.

In considering the case construction of the upright pianoforte, we are led to observe that this type exhibits, in these matters, certain important advantages over the grand. It is true that the case is not so homogeneously fitted into the resonant structure, and it is equally true that the grand has hitherto had much the better of it in the fight for tonal quality and volume. Nevertheless, considering the upright in the light of its own peculiar fitness for popular use, we are bound to observe, in considering the construction of its case and back-framing, the special advantages over the grand that we mentioned as existing.

The chief and most obvious of the inherent advantages of the upright pianoforte lies in the position which the instrument takes up. The hammers strike in front of the strings and tend to force them down upon the bridges, so that the full energy of the blow is impressed upon them. Further, there is none of that tendency of the strings to fly off from the belly bridge which is always present in the square and to a certain extent in the grand. Again the vertical position of the sound-board would seem to be more favorable to the free vibration of the wooden fibres of which it is composed; while the simplicity of the general outline of the upright permits the employment of a larger sound-board area than is possible with either the square or the small grand. Lastly, the wrest-plank is greatly strengthened by the omission of the gap between it and the sound-board, which permits the use of lighter framing and a consequent gain in portability.

While recognizing these facts, however, we are bound to recognize many other features that go far to destroy the great initial advantage here described. It cannot be doubted that today the upright is pre-eminently the popular type. Whether this fact is entirely a matter for congratulation is doubtful, for the upright form lends itself readily to cheap and trashy production. The conditions of modern domestic life are such, on the other hand, that the portability and convenience of the popular type, no less than the possibility of producing it cheaply, have given it a hold upon the public fancy which its own inherent and undoubted advantages might never have secured for it.

The upright form is capable of the highest artistic and mechanical development, and there is no good reason why it should not be so improved as to produce tones equal in volume, purity and richness to those of the grand.

In considering the details of back and case construction in the upright, we are compelled to observe instances of faulty method. For example, it is usual to fasten the sides of the case to the back by gluing after the latter has been fitted with the sound-board, iron frame and strings. This method is obviously faulty. It is not difficult to understand that, although the back partially sustains the tensions imposed by the strings, the sides when glued to the former are constantly subjected to a modification of these tensions. Now, gluing, while convenient, is not the best possible process to give to the sides the necessary strength to bear such strains, for it is a familiar fact that pianofortes that are not of the highest class invariably develop in the course of a few years, more or less serious cracks and breaks in the continuity of the joins between the glued surfaces. When this happens, the equilibrium of the instrument is disturbed and its strength diminished. In addition, the breaks in continuity have, of course, a serious effect upon the power of resonance. Furthermore, the glue method is subject to various mechanical defects. It is absolutely necessary that the surfaces that are to be united should be maintained, during the process of gluing, at an absolutely uniform temperature. And this temperature must be high. Consequently it is not hard to see that in the haste and confusion of construction in the factory, the large sides and backs may not be so carefully handled as to insure the continual maintenance of the ideal temperature conditions. If, in short, the surfaces to be glued together are permitted to become cold, it is obvious that the adhesion will be imperfect, that the wear and tear of constant usage will complete what carelessness in the factory began, and that the value of the instrument will be permanently impaired.

Before suggesting a remedy for these regrettable conditions, or a substitute for the faulty methods described, it will be well to examine carefully the principles that underlie the construction of the upright pianoforte back. It will thus become less difficult to find some better method of uniting the sides and back, so as better to conserve the strength and durability of the instrument.

The back of the upright pianoforte might almost be considered as the foundation of the instrument. Indeed, before the general introduction of iron framing, this part of the construction deserved such a description. Its position, however, is now somewhat subordinate, since the wooden framing of which it is composed is quite inadequate to the task of supporting the tension of the strings. As generally built, this back consists of a number (usually six) of wooden posts arranged in an upright position and joined at the top and bottom by braces, also of wood and of similar dimensions. Thus is provided a compact frame that may be made to possess great strength and resisting power. But, in order to accomplish properly the duties for which it is designed, the construction of this frame must be very carefully planned and carried out. At its upper end it must give proper support to the wrest-plank and the sound-board must rest easily and securely within its embrace. The iron frame must then be fastened upon and over the structure.

It would be absurd to suppose that the back is not subjected to modifications of the strains imposed upon the sound-board, wrest-plank, and iron frame, and it is equally certain that carelessness in working out the details of construction will tend materially to reduce the coefficient of resistance.

An important detail is the joining of the upright posts to the top and bottom rails. If these rails are made continuous and the posts are tenoned into them, the frame will possess the maximum of strength that is possible to such a structure, and if, in addition, the joints are at all places made more secure by the use of screws and other devices as supplements to the gluing, then we may consider that we have a properly made back.

Unfortunately, however, examination of any considerable number of pianofortes of various makes will soon convince the reader that these details of construction are seldom given enough attention. Many instruments will be found to have the back posts joined at top and bottom by short pieces of wood which do not extend further than the two posts which each unites. Such a method of construction, especially when combined with careless gluing and an absence of other fastenings, provides a frame that possesses none of the desiderata of homogeneity, compactness and strength.

BACK VIEW OF UPRIGHT PIANOFORTE, KNABE PATENTS, SHOWING RIBBING OF SOUND-BOARD AND CONSTRUCTION OF BACK FRAMING.

The upright wrest-plank differs somewhat from the synonymous structure used in the grand. It does not suffer under the disadvantage of an involuntary and inevitable separation from the sound-board and the lower portion of the back, but, when constructed with a due regard for correct principles, forms one homogeneous and uniform structure. The upright wrest-plank should, therefore, possess rigidity and resisting power of the highest order, and should form an unyielding support for the tuning-pins. The general construction of such a wrest-plank will not differ materially from that which has already been discussed in reference to the grand pianoforte. That is to say, the building up of the body of the structure from crossed layers of hard maple and the bolting of it into the iron frame (when the latter is made so as to extend over the whole surface of the back frame) will be done in the same way. But the upright wrest-plank derives from the peculiar form of construction that is proper to the upright pianoforte a further element of strength that is lacking in the grand. For it is in direct and solid connection with the sound-board and the other parts of the back-framing, and thus obtains a considerable addition of strength. Indeed, the wrest-plank should be so constructed as to form an integral part of the top rail of the back, and should be, in fact, the front portion of this rail. Further, its connection with the rest of the back-frame should be as close and binding as possible, and it is most essential that a sufficient number of lag screws should be driven into the wrest-plank and through the latter into the further and remote parts of the back-frame top-rail.

Having thus analyzed the construction of the back in all its parts and divisions, we may return to the discussion of the sides of the case and the best methods of uniting them with the back. The reader has now a good working knowledge of the construction, prior to the putting on of the sides, and he cannot have failed to come to the conclusion that gluing is a poor method for joining heavy sides to the elaborate structure known as the back. Nor does there seem to be any good practical reason why some other method should not be substituted for the antiquated gluing. There is no good mechanical reason why a system of screws should not be devised that would not only not mar the outer appearance of the case, but also afford a more certain and secure manner of uniting the sides to the rest of the instrument. Moreover, such a method would largely increase portability by making possible the removal of the sides when conditions of transport required this. Manufacturers might profitably spend a little time in estimating the saving that a detachable side would enable them and the dealers to effect in their annual shipping and trucking bills.

The various sizes of upright pianofortes that are customarily found range from nearly five feet in height down to about ten inches less. Some very small models are made no more than four feet high. But the public appears to prefer the larger styles, and in this they are entirely right. For the very small pianofortes, no matter how cunningly they be scaled, cannot be equipped with strings of the proper lengths, nor with sound-boards of sufficient area. Hence their tonal possibilities are very limited. The full sized upright, on the other hand, approaches closely to the tonal excellence of the grand.

The styles of case decoration that are and have been applied to the upright are even more striking and varied than those of the grand. For the upright lends itself more readily to that kind of decorative treatment that considers the whole case as one single entity, and thus harmoniousness of design and unity of treatment are more easily obtained. At the same time, we are bound to confess that the outline of the upright is essentially box-like, and that this defect operates continually to nullify the efforts of the designer to conceal it. It is a fact that over-elaboration of decorative treatment is usually accompanied by most unfortunate effects; while the larger styles 77 at least are little adapted to sustain the burden of meretricious exterior adornment. In fact, we may well say that the upright is decoratively at its best in the small sizes. Since, however, there is a public demand for large models, which are indeed mechanically and acoustically superior, we must be content to observe the progress of decorative ideas as applied to the beautifying of these.

One of the most striking features of the modern decorative movement, as applied to furniture, is seen in the great popularity of rare and beautiful woods. These are much prized, and it has come to be popular to finish them in such a manner as plainly to exhibit the natural figurings and markings. We have even seen a craze for plain rubbing with wax, which leaves the wood in absolutely its natural appearance. Red and White Mahogany, Burled and Circassian Walnut, Satin Wood, Bird's-Eye Maple, Golden and Flemish Oak, and many other beautiful and costly varieties are constantly made up into rich and elaborate pieces of furniture. In this development the upright has had a large part. While the large size and great first cost of the grand has made the purchasing of specially decorated cases a matter to be avoided by all except the wealthy, the same obstacle has not so largely existed to frighten away the artistic would-be-purchaser of an upright. In fact, the decorative movement has shown its best manifestations through the medium of the upright pianoforte, and this in spite of the unfortunate outline of the instrument that resists all efforts to conceal its excessive crudity.

Models of the English schools have been produced with great success, and the inlaying of rich woods, after the manner of Chippendale, has resulted in some very beautiful specimens of this particular art. Again, we find the so-called Renaissance, the Colonial, the Empire (more elaborate than the other two), the Doric (severely simple), and last but not least, the Mission. The latter, extraordinary perversion of the handicraft of the Spanish fathers as it usually is found to be, has nevertheless been the cause of one great good. It has begun to popularize the dull finish, and to teach the public that the high, glassy, fragile, and unreliable varnish finish is not the only possible way of putting a surface upon wood. The Mission craze has taught many people to admire the natural figure and markings of a fine veneer or piece of lumber, without regard to the fact that it is or is not covered with a mirror-like finish that cracks as soon as the room becomes cold.

In fact we may discern the encouraging signs of a growing sanity and refinement in the demand for, and production of, suitable designs for the decorative treatment of pianoforte cases. It has come to be recognized that a truly chaste and beautiful exterior is the fitting complement to richness and nobility of tone. The growth of this feeling deserves the highest encouragement from all. American makers may well congratulate themselves upon being the foremost exponents of this movement.

CHAPTER X.
THE IRON FRAME OF THE PIANOFORTE.

In the historical portion of the present work, ample reference has been made to the genesis and early development of metallic framing in the construction of pianofortes. We took occasion to point out that the independent development of the American pianoforte is intimately connected with the rise and improvement of the system. It is a matter of no little pride to recall that in the universal recognition of the value of metallic adjuncts to the framing devices of the modern pianoforte, the Americans, as became their traditions, blazed the trail. It is unnecessary to repeat the observations that were made in Chapter II as to the controversies that have raged over the question of priority of invention. It is sufficient to refer the reader back to that portion of the present work where these questions have been treated in a sufficiently copious manner.

We may therefore proceed directly to the task of investigating the nature of the universal metallic framing that has been demonstrated to be so essential in modern constructional systems. Following the plan that we have adopted throughout, we shall first consider the nature and application of this kind of framing to the grand pianoforte.

As to the form, then, of the iron framing, its weight and size. Ever since the first grand pianoforte was produced with an iron plate cast in one piece, designers have been busy with attempts to improve upon the original invention. They have met with but moderate success. There have been multifarious changes in the details of bracing and of fitting the plate to the case, but the general form of the original design remains the same. It may be described in general terms as follows: A plate of iron cast in one piece, which follows the outline of the instrument and is so arranged that it may be secured to the case and to the wooden framing that underlies and knits together the latter and the sound-board. A gap is left in this plate at the point where the hammers strike the strings, and the resultant weakness is overcome by a system of bracing by means of resistance bars, also of iron and cast in the same piece with the main body. At its front end, nearest to the key-board, the plate is extended so as to cover the wrest-plank in which are driven the tuning-pins; and at the end remote from the key-board it is provided with a number of hitch-pins, to which are secured the waste ends of the strings. This plate, further, is so arranged that the sound-board is not covered by it except at the edges, and at the place where the bass bridge is constructed another gap is left in its surface.

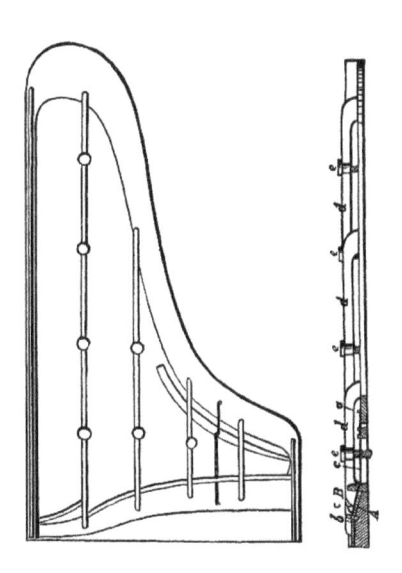

JONAS CHICKERING'S FULL SOLID CAST GRAND METAL PLATE.

The above general description comprehends in bare outline the essential features of the iron framing. There are, of course, many variations of detail, and in seeking for the best methods of designing this important part of the pianoforte we shall have occasion to examine the greater number of these with some care.

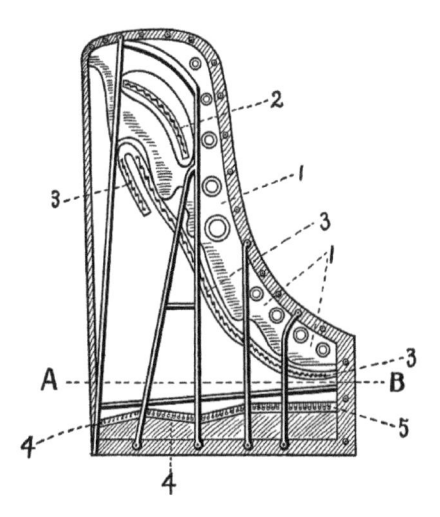

SKETCH OF IRON PLATE FOR CONCERT GRAND, SHOWING GENERAL ARRANGEMENT OF BRACES, BELLY-BRIDGES AND SYSTEM OF BOLTS FOR FASTENING TO CASE.

- **A—B. Hammer line.**
- **1. Body of plate.**
- **2. Bass bridge.**
- **3. Continuous treble bridge.**
- **4. Agraffes.**
- **5. Capo d'astro bar.**

Plate is cast in one piece and scale is overstrung.

Of the various differences of detail that designers have effected in the construction of iron framing, one of the most important is presented in the so-called "cupola" style of construction. In this form the surface of the plate is raised at the edges of the case in such a manner as to give the general outline of a cupola or semi-dome. The result of this method is to increase the resonance of the framing and, at the same time, greatly to enhance the tensile strength of the whole construction. The "cupola" style was the subject of a patent by Steinway & Sons of New York some years ago, but has been extensively copied since that time. The same celebrated house was the originator of another variation upon the classic manner of plate building. Instead of arranging the strings in the usual manner, a fan-like disposition was adopted, with the result of distributing the strain more evenly throughout the entire surface and thus improving the tensile qualities of the whole plate. All these methods of construction, however, have failed to avoid that breaking up of the scale which is made necessary by the interposition, between the string groups, of bars and bracings. It has appeared impossible to obtain the requisite resisting power without the assistance of a number of heavy iron braces cast into the plate and designed to increase the tensile strength, which is weakened by the gap at the striking points of the hammers.

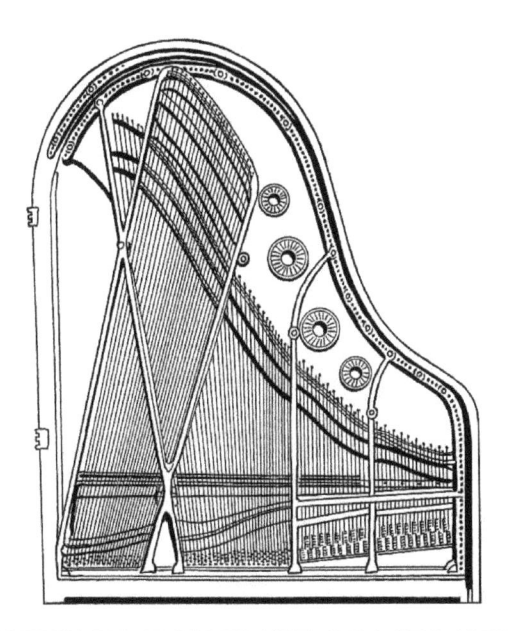

ARRANGEMENT OF IRON PLATE, BRACES AND SCALE OF PARLOR SIZE GRAND PIANOFORTE.

There has, however, appeared an invention which would seem to overcome, in an effective manner, the objections to a multiplication of bracings. The inventor is a member of the celebrated house of Broadwood, and his device is called the "Barless" or "open scale" grand pianoforte. By this invention the barred iron frame is replaced by a plate of mild steel, which is entirely free from bracings, is constructed with a continuous turned-up flange and is bolted in the usual manner into the bottom framing. This flange provides the necessary tensile strength and apparently sustains the tension of the strings in a perfectly satisfactory manner. The advantages presented by a method of construction that avoids the breaking up of the string groups into three or four divisions are obvious and need not be explained in detail.

It may be stated, however, that the principal and conspicuous advantage presented by this method of construction is found in the fact that the absence of the usual barring and bracing tends to subdue the metallic and tinkling quality of tone that is so often found to be induced by the presence of heavy masses of cast iron. At the same time, the material employed is so much more elastic than iron that there is no perceptible loss of resonance, nor is the tensile strength lessened to any appreciable degree. No one who has tested the pianofortes thus constructed has failed to be delighted with the singularly beautiful tone-quality and remarkable evenness that is shown throughout the whole compass. It is indeed a most difficult task to overcome the tendency to production of unduly prominent dissonant partials in those parts of the scale where the bracing is especially heavy, particularly in the lower portions, and consequently we must regard with admiration so successful an attempt to do away with these difficulties by removing their cause.

It may be noted at this point that the eminent firm referred to before as having introduced the "cupola" form of construction, also employ steel in the making of their metal frames, and it seems curious that this example has not been more generally followed.

The two types thus described are the most radical exceptions to the common style of metal framing. It is a matter of regret that manufacturers in general have been content to follow so closely in the footsteps of the pioneers, and have not experimented more energetically with a view to effecting other improvements in the accepted methods. The problem of sustaining the necessary tensions would undoubtedly be simplified by the adoption, at least in part, of the ideas of the eminent firms who have already been mentioned.

In order thoroughly to understand the actual advantages and disadvantages of the various styles of framing that have been described, we must consider how great are the tensions that they are compelled to bear. A concert grand pianoforte of a standard American make is so constructed that it bears a total strain, when tuned at concert pitch, of not less than 30 tons. The requirements of increased tone and the weight and bulk of strings tend constantly to augment rather than to decrease these tremendous strains, and at the same time more and more to induce the production of those dissonant partials that have such a maleficent influence upon tone-quality. Obviously, then, if we are to satisfy the popular demand for greater volume, and at the same time to maintain the highest standards of quality, we must seek for some method that will obviate the employment of yet heavier masses of cast iron and at the same time preserve the necessary strength and rigidity. The methods of construction that have been noticed at some length above seem to present manifold advantages over the older styles. Steel has greater tensile strength than iron, and consequently a smaller bulk of it is required. Again, its elasticity is higher and the vibrations impressed upon it traverse its surface with greater facility and in a shorter period of time. Whether, therefore, we prefer the barless or the cupola style of construction, we must recognize the fact that steel is a better material than iron in any form.

Foremost among the requirements of a successful framing system are that it shall sustain its burden with such rigidity that the strings shall stand in tune and the wooden case of the instrument shall not be twisted out of shape. Even if the material be the best possible, a faulty method of securing the metal frame to the case will not only prevent the consummation of these desires, but will tend to weaken the sound-board and hasten its splitting. It is essential, in fact, that the board should be relieved of strain, and great care must therefore be exercised in fitting the framing. The approved method is as follows: The framing is connected with the system of wooden posts that extend below the sound-board and bind together the sides of the case. The latter connection is made by means of long bolts that extend through the bracings of the frame and are sunk into the posts at convenient places. The sound-board is secured to the sides of the case by means of its ribs, which are continued beyond its edges and pocketed into the sides and the posts, and also by being glued to the bottom surface of the case and to the system of posts. Lastly, the frame is connected both with the board and the posts, by a series of heavy screws that pass through the board and into the posts at regular intervals along its outer edges.

This method of securing the frame and sound-board to the case ensures that the former shall be incorporated within the body of the instrument as rigidly as is possible, and that the latter shall have the fullest protection against those twisting strains that the metal frame alone ought to bear.

With such a method as has been described we can find no great fault. It should be noted, however, that in the barless or open scale construction the bolts that were described as passing through the braces into the posts below are omitted, and the whole frame is supported within the case by a series of bolts driven through the turned-up steel flange at equal intervals in its surface.

Having thus considered the forms of framing that are employed by various makers we may turn our attention to the matter of suspending the strings across the frame and over the sound-board. The upward stroke of the hammer of the grand pianoforte tends to drive the string away from its bridge and thus to lessen the energy with which the vibrations imparted to the string are impressed upon the latter. We may note that all makers are agreed in giving to the strings of a grand pianoforte an upward thrust or "bearing" in order that the blow of the hammer may throw the strings against the upper surface of the bearing-bridge instead of away from it. There are two devices that are generally employed for this purpose. They are known as the "agraffe" and the "capo d'astro bar."

The first of these was the invention of the celebrated Erard of Paris. It consists of a brass stud screwed into the iron framing (or into the wrest-plank where the plate does not extend over the latter), at the beginning of the speaking length of each string or group of strings. This stud is bored with the required number of holes—one for each string in the group. These holes are bored at such an angle that the ends nearest to the tuning-pins are higher than the other ends, while the pins are placed at a higher elevation than the agraffes. In this manner the string is given an upward thrust as it proceeds toward the tuning-pin, and the blows of the hammer force it against the upper surface of the agraffe, which, being solid, conveys the impressed vibrations through the medium of its own surface to the framing.

The "capo d'astro bar" performs the same functions in a slightly different manner. It is practically a continuous "agraffe," and consists of a metal bar which is cast into the metal frame at the beginning of the speaking length of the strings. It is fitted, according to the best practice, with an under edge of tool steel, and the strings are caused to pass underneath it on their way toward the tuning-pins, which are higher than the bar, as before. The up-bearing is thus imparted to the strings in a manner similar to that which is followed in the case of the agraffes.

As to the advantages of the two systems, it may be said that the "capo d'astro" undoubtedly overcomes those objections to agraffes which are based upon their tendency to pull out from their places. It provides an absolutely rigid resistance, and is therefore stronger and more reliable.

On the other hand, however, the mass of metal employed is considerably greater than in the "agraffe" method, and the resultant influences upon tone-quality are clearly disadvantageous.

Further, the work of tuning is rendered more difficult by reason of the fact that the strings cannot so readily and correctly be pulled through the space intervening between the bar and the tuning-pin. It is debatable whether the greater rigidity and resonance offered by the "capo d'astro" method are not too dearly bought at the cost of inconvenience in tuning and deterioration of tone-quality. It is noteworthy that most manufacturers confine the "capo d'astro" bar to the high treble register of their instruments, where brilliancy and a somewhat metallic quality of tone are a desideratum.

The iron framing of an upright piano follows the same general lines of construction as have already been noted in the previous discussion of the grand. The functions of the frame are precisely the same and its construction differs outwardly but little. There are, however, certain divergencies from the grand forms that must be noted carefully. For example, it will be remembered that the form of the upright pianoforte is such that the framing has no direct and positive connection with the outside case. It is thus impracticable to consider the sides of the iron plate as homogeneous with the sides of the case, nor is it possible to give to it that consistency of form that, in the grand, results from the shaping of the plate to correspond with the curved outline of the case. This, however, is no reason why the upright iron plate should not be as strong and secure as that of the grand.

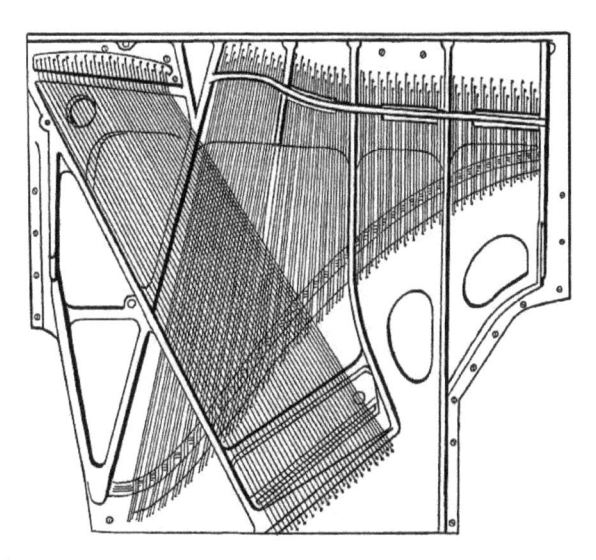

IRON PLATE FOR UPRIGHT PIANOFORTE FITTED WITH CAPO D'ASTRO BAR.

Among the various differences of detail that we observe to exist between these two forms of plate is the device adopted to secure the bearing and rigidity of the strings at their upper end deserves notice. The practice is entirely different in this respect as regards the upright, and we are therefore introduced to a new feature: the "pressure bar." This device has superseded both the old-fashioned pinned bearing bridge and the later agraffe forms. It consists, essentially, of a bar of heavy metal that is screwed into the wrest-plank through the metal plate and is placed so that the strings pass under it on the way to the tuning pins. In fact it occupies the same position as do the agraffes or capo d'astro bar on the grand. Its function is also similar; namely, accurately to delimit the speaking lengths of the strings at the upper end and to assist in the formation of a thrust or bearing whereby the latter may more advantageously be secured.

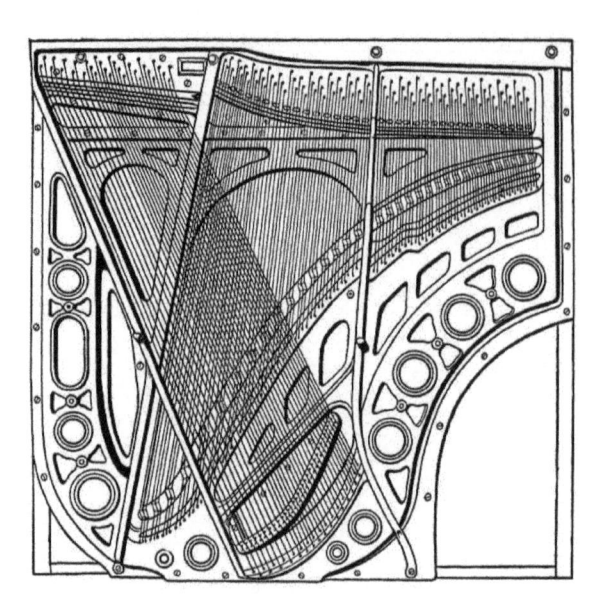

IRON PLATE FOR UPRIGHT PIANOFORTE WITH AGRAFFES (MEHLIN PATENTS).

This form of building the bearing bridge possesses important advantages. It does not require to be cast into the plate, nor is it weakened, as in the agraffe system, by being broken up into a large number of units. Moreover, the bearing for the strings is formed much more smoothly and easily between the pressure bar and its attendant ribs on the plate than is possible when either the agraffes or the capo d'astro bar are used. This is an important point, for such construction tends to make the task of tuning much more rapid and correct.

There are, however, several points to be considered in the designing of pressure bars. As a general thing, it is impracticable to apply this form to the bass strings on account of the fact that the overstringing requires of them a slanting direction. On this account the pressure bar cannot be made properly to maintain the obliquely-running strings in their respective places. It is therefore usual to build the bass bridge after the old pinned type and thus to secure the bass strings by much the same device as is employed in the belly bridges.

As far as the designing of pressure bars is concerned, it will be found that care should be exercised in arranging the space that the bar must occupy and its position with regard to the scale ribs that are placed on each side of it and that support the strings before and after their passage under it. In general it may be said that the pressure bar must be screwed in such a position that its lower curved surface is lower than the upper surfaces of the scale ribs by about one-half of the height of the latter. It must also describe a curve that corresponds to the dip or angle of the scale and must be secured by enough screws (one between each three string-groups is usual), to ensure that the pull of the strings will have no injurious effect upon its rigidity. It is also essential that the curve into which the string is bent during its passage under the pressure-bar and over the scale-ribs be not too deep or sudden. The bearing surface of the bar should be gently rounded until very near its middle point where the string exercises its greatest pulling strain. Here the surface must be curved a little more sharply.

The iron plate of the upright is the chief supporter of the strains imposed upon the structure by the strings. It is necessary, as in the grand, that it should be built so as to have absolute rigidity under these strains, and that it should be always capable of withstanding any others that may by any chance be imposed upon it. Remembering this, what shall we say of the designs that we sometimes see where the iron is cut and shaved away at every possible point in order to save a few pounds of weight? There are pianofortes in existence where the iron framing is so much cut down that the treble can never be depended upon to stay in tune for a reasonable length of time, and where the unevenness of the distribution of metal throughout the body of the frame has caused a warping of the whole instrument out of its proper shape. All this is unnecessary, but it will continue so long as manufacturers are willing to effect small savings at the expense of the future reliability of their product.

It is certainly much better to have the plate of the upright pianoforte so arranged that the total volume of iron, if it is to be decreased, may have this process applied evenly and all through. The most correct design would consider a moderately heavy plate of iron, or better, of steel. This plate would be so arranged that the hitch-pin plate (the portion which carries the hitch-pins) covers the entire surface of the instrument at its bottom end and is bolted into the back with as many and as heavy bolts as are employed at the other end. The upper portion of the proposed plate need not extend over the surface of the wrest-plank, for such a construction can add little to the resisting power of the frame, while it inevitably tends, for reasons that have already been described, to the production of dissonant partials and the consequent emission of a metallic tone. If it is desirable, for any reason, to cut down the weight of a frame, it can better be done at the upper end than at the lower, where diminution of the resisting power of the frame is most severely felt.

We may, then, contemplate a form of iron frame which covers that portion of the back-framing whereon the edges of the sound-board are glued, and that is not continued up and over the wrest-plank. It will be cut away in the centre, as in the grand, and will thus expose a large part of the sound-board to view. It will be provided with a certain number of bracings for the purpose of taking up the strains that are imposed upon the structure at the points of greatest resistance, such as those where the over-stringing begins and ends, and those around the middle registers of the scale. There must not be more of these bracings, however, than is necessary, as it is very important that the scale should be broken up into the least possible number of divisions. The bracings will be so designed that no one of them interferes with the true curve of the belly-bridge. The whole structure will be solidly bolted into the back-framing through the sound-board by a series of long and heavy screws and bolts that will be inserted at frequent intervals along the edges.

We cannot conclude this survey of plate-construction without taking note of a property that is common to all cast-iron structures. We refer to shrinkage. The calculations of the designer, no matter how carefully worked out, must take into consideration the fact that cast-iron shrinks largely in the cooling. It must be noted that the design for the iron plate is the chief portion of the work of scale draughting. As will be explained later on, this work is first done on paper and then transferred to a wooden pattern. From this pattern the casting is made. After the first casting is thus completed it is taken in hand by the designer, who marks and punches it for the boring and pinning and corrects it where necessary. The corrected casting is then used as a model for the future plates that are to be turned out for the same scale. But these also shrink; so that we are compelled to take into account both shrinkages, and allow for each. Fortunately, however, there is no difficulty in arranging this.

The method is as follows: After the string-lengths have been calculated and the size of the iron plate thus determined, a complete drawing is made, showing the exact dimensions, shape, and other features of the proposed plate. This is to be used as the guide for the wooden templet. But this difference exists between the two paper drawings; namely, that the second is multiplied as to every dimension of the plate by a quantity that represents the amount of shrinkage that is known to occur in the two castings.

The average shrinkage of cast-iron in the form of pianoforte plates is estimated at about one per cent. Consequently to account for the double shrinkage it becomes necessary to multiply by the square of $^{101}/_{100}$; that is approximately $^{51}/_{50}$.

A great deal of trouble will be avoided if the shrinkage is carefully worked out in this manner. Every dimension of the plate is affected, and the greatest care must be taken to ensure that the corrected calculations are accurate. Only thus will it be possible for the ideas of the designer to be brought out in the completed instrument as he expects to see them.

CHAPTER XI.
THE MECHANISM OF PERCUSSION.

The pianoforte hammer is perhaps the most striking of the many and various features of that instrument. Although it is a comparatively simple device, its historical and musical interest is supreme. For while the strings, the framing, and even the action that we see in the instruments of today are but the modern developments of their clavichord and harpsichord ancestors, the hammer, on the contrary, is the one revolutionary device that, at a single step, separated the pianoforte from all other stringed instruments and endowed it with its own peculiar and powerful attributes.

It was the hammer, in fact, that made the pianoforte. As soon as it was fitted into a harpsichord, the pianoforte was born, and no refinement of stringing or framing could have effected the fundamental nature of key-board instruments in the same manner. For we must recognize the fact, sometimes overlooked, that the pianoforte is essentially an instrument of percussion. It is necessary that there be a more or less violent blow from the hammer to excite the sound-producing vibrations of the strings. The tone of the instrument, under the most favorable circumstances, cannot fail to partake of the character peculiar to sounds produced in this manner. The importance of the hammer as a tone-producer cannot, then, be underestimated. It stands upon a plane of importance equal to that occupied by the scale-designing, the stringing and the resonance apparatus. We are therefore justified in devoting space to consideration of the construction of this essential feature.

We cannot say with absolute surety what was the nature of the material with which the hammers of Cristofori's original invention were covered. But we may presume that it was leather. We know that the hammers were exceedingly small and apparently all of the same size. Neither Silbermann nor Zumpe can be said to have perfected any special improvements in the form of hammer construction, and we find that the revolutionary genius, John Broadwood the First, and also Sebastian Erard, were the pioneers in the work of adapting the hammers to the more strenuous styles of playing that the improved touch mechanism invented by them permitted and encouraged.

Broadwood, who first perceived the necessity of adopting a scientifically correct striking point, likewise began to fit his pianofortes with hammers graduated in size, and under him the leather-covered hammer arrived at its full development.

But leather as a covering material soon began to be decried. It was discovered that the kind of tone demanded by the rising pianoforte masters could not be obtained from such material. After much experiment on the part of pianoforte makers, the German-Frenchman, Pape, of Paris, tried the use of felt. His success was immediate and conspicuous, and it was discovered that not only did this kind of covering produce finer tone quality, but there was little difficulty in regulating that quality through the hammers within certain well-defined limits. Nevertheless, we find square pianofortes to-day in which the felt covering upon the higher hammers is overlaid with strips of buckskin. This practice, however, represented the last dying struggles of the leather-covered hammer, and now we use it no longer.

It is true that the use of felt is not unattended with conspicuous disadvantages. It wears out rapidly, and unless constantly kept in good condition by use of the felt-needles, the iron, and the sand-paper file, soon comes to produce a harsh and unpleasant tone-quality. This defect arises from the fact that as usually constructed, the continual pounding of the hammer head upon the strings causes the felt on the crown of the hammer head to become tightly packed and compressed, and the shaping of the head to be lost. As will be explained later, this change in the manner in which the head is originally made up causes a modification in the nature of the vibrations set up in the strings, and, as we have already learned, this change in the nature of the produced excitement is the cause of unpleasant tone-quality. Nevertheless, and in spite of these real disadvantages, the use of felt as a covering material for pianoforte hammers is now universal. Nor does it seem at present that we are very likely to find a superior substitute. As we shall shortly see, however, a simple change in the manner of securing the felt to the wooden foundation of the hammer-head may be depended upon to add largely to the durability and efficiency of the whole structure, both as a tone-producing medium and as a mechanical device.

As will be surmised by the reader, early covering of pianoforte hammers with felt was a tedious operation. The material was cut up separately for each hammer, and glued on to the wooden head by hand. But this method suffered under the grave disadvantage of affording no correct guide to the true thicknesses and no means other than furnished by hand-cutting, of graduating these thicknesses with exact evenness. It remained for an American (or Americanized German) inventor to devise a machine that should glue up and finish an entire set of hammers from one continuous sheet of felt, of which the thickness was graduated in the making and which could be relied upon to contain the correct amount of felt, of any desired total weight, the whole graduated with great evenness. Not merely was this so, but the methods of manufacturing felt for other special purposes connected with the manufacture of pianofortes has been entirely revolutionized, so that today we have dampers, punchings, and many other parts of the mechanism of pianofortes successfully manufactured out of various kinds of felt, which vary greatly in consistency, thickness, and other properties.

To return, however, to the special case of hammer-felt. We find that the original methods of working together the layers of carded wool has been much improved, chiefly through the efforts of the inventor mentioned above. It is now a matter of slight difficulty to turn out sheets of felt for the making of piano hammers that shall have any desired weight, size and graduation of thickness.

The weight of the sheets of felt varies largely according to the nature of the hammers that are to be produced. Thus it is customary, as may be guessed, to provide full-size concert grands with hammers of greater thickness, while the smaller styles of instrument have progressively smaller hammers. The actual weights vary according to the caprice or calculation of manufacturers and designers. An average weight of felt for hammers suitable to be placed in a nine-foot concert grand is from 16 to 18 lbs. per sheet. This does not include the "underfelt," which is glued directly to the wooden head of the hammer and is used to give greater resiliency to the lower hammers. It is generally omitted at the higher treble end.

Upright pianofortes frequently are hammered with felt weighing not more than 8 lbs. to the sheet, but this seems to be too light for really efficient results. 10 lbs. is quite light enough in most cases.

As has already been indicated, the foundation of the hammer is a wooden molding. Over this is glued, in the machine, a strip of "underfelt," which is long enough to cover about five and a half or six octaves of hammers, counting from the bass end upwards. The main felting is then laid over this, the thickest end being at the lowest bass. By means of the machines, now so generally used, it is possible to glue the entire underfelt and also the topäfelt, in one piece. The moldings are then separated and the operation is complete. It is customary to insert a small piece of wire, doubled over in a loop, through each hammer, in order to ensure further strength to the fastening.

As may well be imagined, the details of manufacture, of the quality of the felting, and of the dimensions of the completed hammers, require much care in their execution. Long practice, study, and experience have combined to render the specialists, who devote themselves to the preparation of hammers and hammer-felt, most excellently fitted to place upon the market the very finest productions of this kind.

There have been attempts made at various times to provide a hammer head, and a method of felting it, that would obviate the somewhat rapid deterioration caused by the pounding of the glued and compressed felt against the stiff steel wire strings. The felt, which requires to be compressed before it is glued on to the wooden molding, rapidly becomes altogether too hard. Moreover, the fastening of the felt to the molding is by no means really permanent. It has been suggested that the felt might properly be contained within a wooden shell which would extend as far along the sides of the felt as the wooden molding now reaches within it. The compressed sheet of felt would be forced into this shell and fastened therein so that it would always be protected by an outer wooden covering. Thus, not only would the fastening of the felt to the wood be reduced more secure, but the pounding upon the strings would not so rapidly assure the undue hardening of the felt. For there would not be the hard wooden base between which the strings and the felt is continually subjected to compression. The idea is good and undoubtedly will yet be recognized.

Details of the adjustment of the hammers to the rest of the action and of the preparation of them by the tone-regulator, for the better production of good and even tone, will be dealt with in the chapters upon action-and tone-regulating.

CHAPTER XII.
THE TOUCH MECHANISM.

As the hammer-idea evolved itself in the mind of Cristofori and the other experimenters who were contemporaneously bending their efforts towards the improvement of the dynamic possibilities of keyed instruments, we may be certain that much perplexity was caused them by the problem of providing some mechanism that should form the connecting link between the hammer and the key. We may understand how the ingenious Italian must have labored, with the picture of the dulcimer and its player continually in his mind, to obtain an efficient mechanical substitute for the uncertain stroke of the hand operated dulcimer-hammer, as well as the dynamically incapable harpsichord jack and quill. It is surprising to note, indeed, how early the present ruling principles of action-mechanism were elaborated by these pioneer workers. Cristofori, as we have already mentioned, obtained, ere he died, a complete check to the rebound of the hammer and a form of escapement that may be seen unaltered in essentials in surviving square pianofortes of the "English action" variety. We may further reflect that the invention of Backers, as improved by John Broadwood the First, remains today the approved mechanism of many English and other European grands. Not only is this so, but until the general adoption of the Steinway overstrung model, there existed German makers who were content to fit their moderate priced grands with a slightly modified form of the Viennese action invented by that remarkable woman Nanette Stein, afterwards Madame Streicher, the conspicuous feature of which was the mobility of the hammer-butt and the stationary condition of the jack. The fact that these early mechanisms remained satisfactory to performers until recent years is the best proof of the thorough and sure mechanical basis upon which they were designed.

It is not necessary to go into elaborate detail in describing these early actions. Reference to the accompanying cuts will be sufficient to lay bare their actuating principles. We may, however, observe that the radical difference of touch between the Viennese (Streicher) models and those of Broadwood (known as the English grand action) continued to be a source of annoyance to performers until the increasing technical demands of the modern virtuoso school and the improvements in wire-drawing and iron casting made inevitable the supersession of the very light Streicher action by the heavier, more durable and more efficient Broadwood English model, which continued in favor until within recent years.

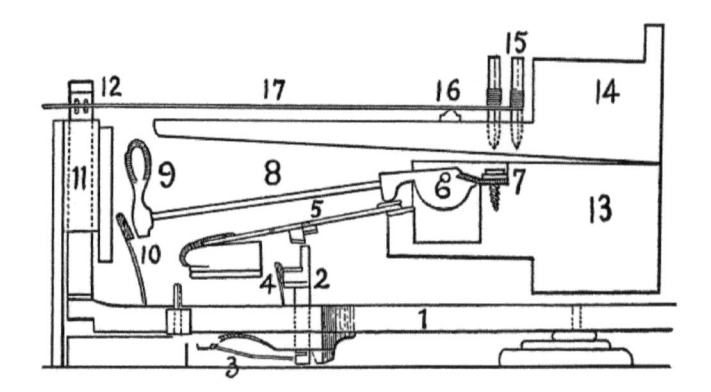

CRISTOFORI'S ACTION IN ITS FINAL FORM.

- 1. Key.
- 2. Jack.
- 3. Jack-operating spring.
- 4. Cushion limiting rebound of jack.
- 5. Under-hammer.
- 6. Hammer-butt.
- 7. Hinge of hammer-butt.
- 8. Hammer-shank.
- 9. Hammer head.
- 10. Check.
- 11. Damper-lifter.
- 12. Damper-head.
- 13. Action-beam.
- 14. Wrest-plank.
- 15. Tuning pins.
- 16. Bearing-bridge.
- 17. String.

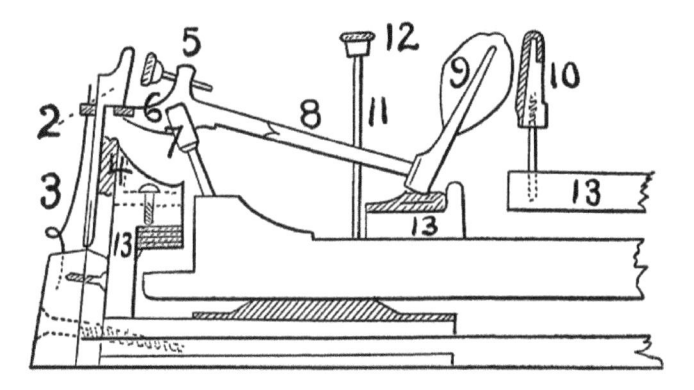

ACTION BY ANDREAS AND NANETTE (STEIN), STREICHER VIENNESE ESCAPEMENT (1794).

- 1. Key.
- 2. Jack.
- 3. Jack-operating spring.
- 4. Cushion limiting rebound of jack.
- 5. Button and screw regulating escapement of hammer.
- 6. Hammer-butt and operating face.
- 7. Hammer-butt pivot.
- 8. Hammer-shank.
- 9. Hammer-head.
- 10. Check.
- 11. Damper-lifter.
- 12. Damper-head.
- 13. Action-rails.

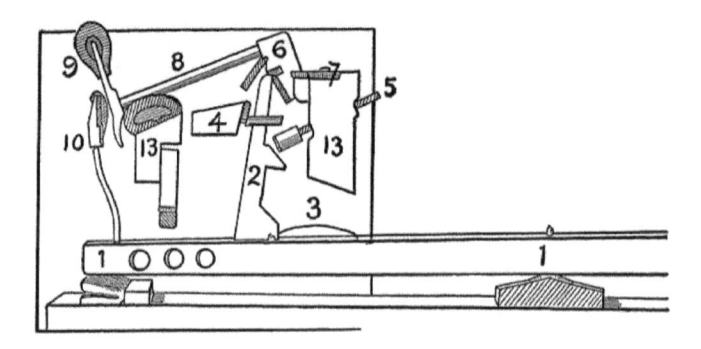

ENGLISH DIRECT LEVER GRAND ACTION, DEVELOPED BY BROADWOOD FROM BACKERS (1884).

- 1. Key.
- 2. Jack.
- 3. Jack operating spring.
- 4. Rail and cushion limiting travel of jack.
- 5. Button and screw regulating escapement of hammer.
- 6. Hammer-butt with operating notch.
- 7. Hammer-butt flange.
- 8. Hammer-shank.
- 9. Hammer-head.
- 10. Check.
- 13. Action-rails.

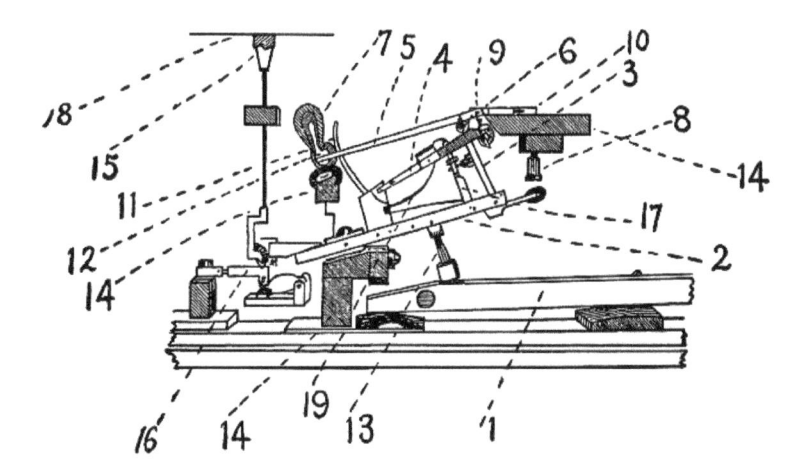

DOUBLE REPETITION ACTION OF SEBASTIAN ERARD AS USED BY S. & P. ERARD, PARIS.

- 1. Key.
- 2. Wippen.
- 3. Jack.
- 4. Escapement lever.
- 5. Hammer-shank.
- 6. Roller.
- 7. Hammer-head.
- 8. Jack regulating button.
- 9. Regulating button to limit rise of escapement lever.
- 10. Hammer-butt.
- 11. Check.
- 12. Felt cushion to engage with check.
- 13. Sticker connecting key and wippen.
- 14. Action-rails.
- 15. Damper-head.
- 16. Damper operating device.
- 17. Device to limit travel of jack.

- **18. String.**
- **19. Spring (v-shaped) for escapement lever and jack.**

Shortly before the general adoption of the Broadwood model, however, there was brought forward a new type of grand action, which was destined in its turn entirely to supersede the then favorite English type. This was the invention of Sebastian Erard, of Paris, founder of the still existing house of S. & P. Erard. His new action was termed the "double repetition action," and it fully deserves the name. By the use of this device the leverage that exists between the hammer and the key is so manipulated that the very slightest touch upon the keys is sufficient to cause the hammer to deliver a blow. It will be observed by reference to the cut that the Erard action differs very largely from that of Broadwood. In the first place, we observe that the hammer heel is no longer provided with a notch in which the jack works, but that this heel is reduced to the smallest dimensions and acts merely as a pivot. Upon the shank of the hammer is fastened a felt-covered roller. The jack acts upon this roller. Between the jack and the roller, however, we observe a long lever, one end of which has a slot through which the jack passes, while the other end is pivoted on to a rail projecting from the wippen. This is the "escapement" or repetition lever, and forms the main improvement of Erard. It will be observed that the repetition lever bears against the roller, and indeed lifts it before the jack can come into engagement with it. The jack, working through the slotted portion of the lever, is not brought into play until the lever has raised the hammer a little way. The long, double spring that acts both upon the lever and the jack gives them their motions, and the result of the depression of the key is that the repetition lever is always in engagement, and when the angular key-motion is not sufficient to bring the jack into play, the work will be done by aid of the lever. Furthermore, the lever operates to maintain the hammer-shank in precisely the proper position for striking, at all times, and without reference to the angular position of the key.

It can easily be understood that such a vital change in action mechanism did not become popular at once. Many pianists objected to double escapement. Notable among these were Chopin and Kalkbrenner; these two being the greatest pianists of their day in Paris. Chopin preferred pianofortes fitted with the Broadwood action.

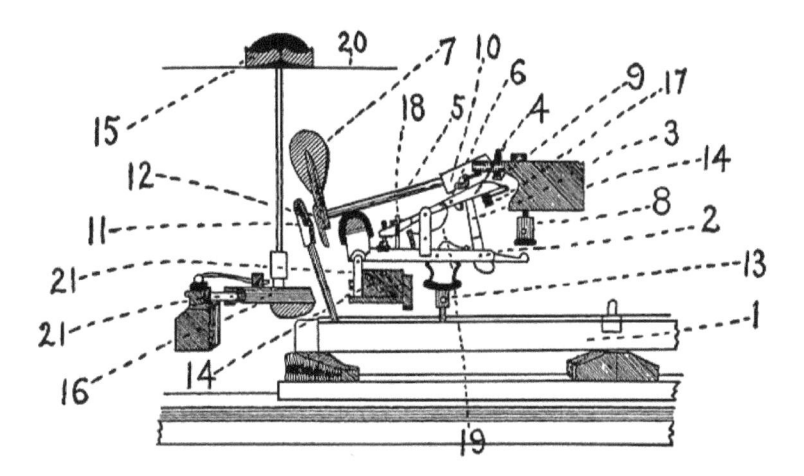

THE ERARD GRAND ACTION MODIFIED BY HERZ.

- 1. Key.
- 2. Wippen.
- 3. Jack.
- 4. Escapement lever.
- 5. Hammer-shank.
- 6. Hammer-butt notch.
- 7. Hammer-head.
- 8. Jack regulating button.
- 9. Regulating button to limit rise of escapement lever.
- 10. Hammer-butt.
- 11. Check.
- 12. Molded tail of hammer-head to engage with check.
- 13. Capstan-screw connecting key and wippen.
- 14. Action-rails.
- 15. Damper-head.
- 16. Damper-operating device.
- 17. Device to limit travel of jack.
- 18. Regulating device for escapement lever.

- **19. Springs (2) for escapement lever and jack.**
- **20. String.**
- **21. Flange.**

Nevertheless, the merits of Erard's invention continued to impress themselves upon the musical world, although Pierre Erard, who had patented his uncle's invention in 1821, was obliged to obtain an extension of the English patent in 1835, on the ground of the loss occasioned in working it. It did not become generally adopted, even after the expiration of the extended patent, until modified and simplified by Henri Herz, the famous pianist and pianoforte manufacturer. Then its merits, in the modified form, were so generally recognized that it is now in use by Steinway, Chickering, Knabe and all manufacturers of grand pianofortes in the United States; by Broadwood, Collard & Collard, Brinsmead, and others in England; by Bechstein & Bluthner in Germany, and by most French makers of eminence with the sole exception of the house of Erard itself. This eminent firm continues to employ the pure and original form of action as patented in 1821, with improvements only in details of workmanship and material.

Whatever we may say as to the general adoption of the Erard action only after it had been considerably modified, we must not withhold admiration from the Erards, whose genius and courage gave to us the enduring double-escapement principle that has never yet been superseded.

The main features of the Herz-Erard mechanism may be seen at a glance. The roller is replaced by the notch, once more restored to favor, and the repetition lever is made more effective by being pivoted centrally with two free ends, and by having means provided to limit its up and down motion. Moreover, the wippen is shortened and made straight, the single spring is replaced by two, and the damper is once more permitted to fall down on the strings by its own weight without recourse to artificial springs.

The Herz-Erard action has been taken up by American makers, but we find that they have modified it again, after their own ideas. For example, if we look at the accompanying cut showing a modern American grand action of the highest class, we shall observe that the original roller of Erard is restored, the damper mechanism simplified and additional means of controlling the movements of the jack introduced. These two latter improvements combine to make the present American grand action most perfect, and the achievements of the specialist action makers must ever command our respectful admiration.

The reader has now been able to take a comparatively complete survey of the progress of invention in grand pianoforte action mechanism. We shall therefore turn to a critical examination of the modern standard grand action here illustrated, in order that the adjustment of it within the instrument may be understood.

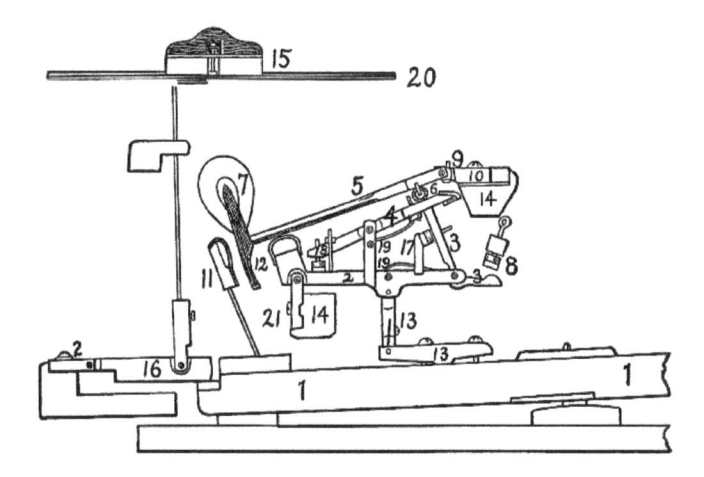

STANDARD MODERN AMERICAN GRAND ACTION.

- 1. Key.
- 2. Wippen.
- 3. Jack.
- 4. Escapement lever.
- 5. Hammer-shank.
- 6. Roller.
- 7. Hammer-head.
- 8. Jack-regulating button.
- 9. Regulating button to limit rise of escapement lever.
- 10. Hammer-butt.
- 11. Check.
- 12. Molded tail of hammer-head to engage with check.
- 13. Key-rocker and sticker connecting wippen and key.
- 14. Action-rails.
- 15. Damper-head.
- 16. Damper operating device.
- 17. Device to limit travel of jack.

- **18. Regulating device for escapement lever.**
- **19. Separate springs for jack and escapement lever.**
- **20. String.**
- **21. Flanges.**

It will be observed that the key (1) is supported upon a key-frame, part of which is clearly shown in the drawing. This frame is provided with a cloth strip at its rear end, also shown, and with a "balance rail" upon which the key is pivoted by means of a pin. The position of this balance rail must be such that the divisions of the key thus made are to one another as 3:2. The part nearest to the player's finger is the longer. But such a proportion as this holds good only for the actual operative lengths of the keys from the front to the point where the sticker, or capstan screw is placed. For otherwise we have a distinct change in the mechanical relations of the parts of the lever-system, and this, of course, entails a corresponding change in the forces that are brought into operation. It is therefore necessary to have a standard length of key, as between the points mentioned, and this length is placed at 15 ¾ inches. But, in order to maintain the mechanical relations between the dimensions of the lever we must also consider the depth to which the key sinks in front, and also the height to which it rises at the back. If, then, we arrange that the depth in front shall be ⅜-inch full and the rise in the rear ¼-inch full, we shall be able to maintain the position of the balance pin as already calculated. Such a proportion supplies the very best arrangement. In order to fix the proportions in the reader's mind we repeat them in tabular form, as follows:

	Inches
Length between front of key and balance pin	9 9/20
Length between balance pin and capstan or sticker	6 3/10
Total length of key between front and capstan or sticker	15 ¾
Depth of fall of front portion of key	⅜ full
Height of rise of back portion of key	¼ full

The front portion of the key is mounted upon a rail of the key-frame which is provided with a pin. This pin works in a mortise cut in the bottom of the front portion of the key and bushed with cloth. The pin is oval in form and adapted to be turned so as partially to increase the amount of space occupied by it whenever wear or age tend unduly to enlarge the size of the mortise.

The exact size of all the various action parts that are mounted above and in connection with the keys depends largely upon the exact interior dimensions of the grand pianoforte case. So that it becomes necessary carefully to measure the height from the key-bed to the level of the strings, and also the distance from the front of the keys to the line of damper lifter wires, and from there to the extreme rear end of the key-bed. Likewise the exact position of the middle string of each three-string group, the middle point of each two-string group and the position of each single string must be marked upon a stick for the guidance of the action-maker. The latter will then be able to effect the correct alignment of the hammers, the rise of the escapement lever and jack, and the exact position, in reference to these, of the other parts of the action. It will, of course, be understood that the proportionate dimensions of all the action parts depend upon the measurements that we mentioned just now, as well as upon the dimensions of the keys. The greatest care is therefore necessary in making these measurements.

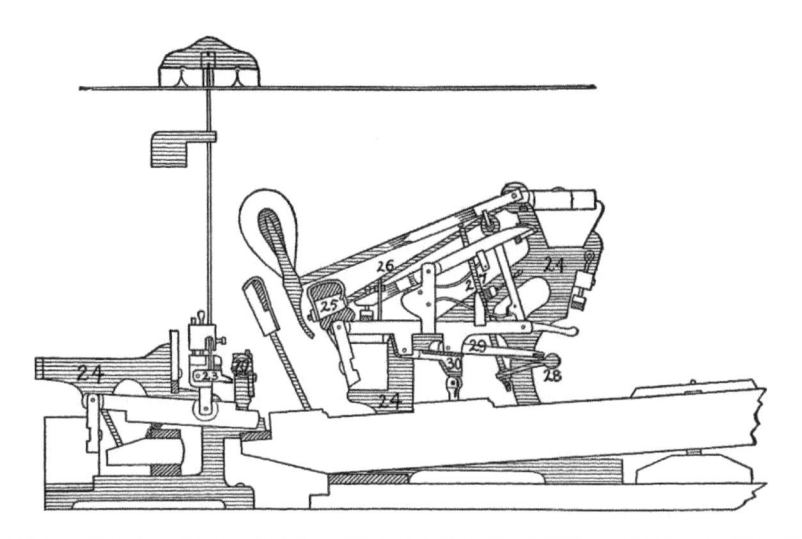

GRAND PIANOFORTE ACTION WITH METALLIC ACTION AND DAMPER FRAMES, SOSTENUTO PEDAL DEVICE AND HAMMER SWINGING SOFT PEDAL ATTACHMENT.

- 22. Sostenuto pedal-rod.
- 23. Attachment to damper-lever engaging with sostenuto pedal-rod.
- 24. Metallic action and damper-brackets.
- 25. Hammer swing-rail and cushion.

- 26. Hammer swing-rail rod.
- 27. Hammer swing-rail lifter.
- 28. Lifter-rod.
- 29. Lost motion compensating levers.
- 30. Lost motion compensating levers.

The junction of these parts with the damper mechanism lies within the province of the action finisher and regulator and will therefore be treated in the chapter on action regulation.

It will be observed then, to return to the consideration of the action in its actual movements, that the depression of the key causes the wippen to rise at its forward end. This brings the escapement lever (4) to bear upon the roller (6), with which it is in continual contact, and raises the hammer-shank and hammer-head (5) and (7). At the same time the jack (3) is raised and its tail end is brought nearer to the button (8), which it finally touches. As soon as this happens the jack is tripped up and its head comes out of contact with the roller. The latter in the meantime, having been raised away from the escapement lever by the action of the jack, falls back into contact with the former and is then borne up on the lever so that the hammer is maintained in position near to the strings. The result of this is that so long as the finger is held on the front of the key, the whole action is continually in proper position to actuate the hammer. The jack is not permitted to fall away, for the roller is maintained in the right place by the escapement lever and it thus happens that a very small angular motion of the key obtained by slightly raising and depressing the finger, is sufficient to cause the whole action to be set in motion, and the operation of actuating the hammer to be gone through as often and as rapidly as required.

The pedal motions of the grand action are simple. The whole action and keys, as we know, are mounted upon the key-frame together, and thus form a homogeneous structure. The *"piano"* pedal is caused to shift this frame so that the hammers each strike only two of the members of each three-string group and only one of each two-string group. This is effected by the use of a heavy spring that is set in the side of the interior case and bears against the key-frame, and by a lever that operates from a hole cut in the bottom of the key-bed and engages with one of the bars of the key-frame. The pedal is connected with this iron lever so as to shift the key-frame, and the spring operates to push the key-frame back into place whenever the foot-pressure is removed from the pedal.

The "*forte*" pedal simply pushes up the whole line of damper levers (16) each of which is pivoted on flanges (21) for that purpose. The lifting is effected by means of a rod connecting with the pedal which is projected through the bottom of the key-bed and engages with a rail set under the line of damper levers and adapted to raise them when operated by the pedal-rod.

There are, however, two variations to the pedal mechanism of grand pianofortes that require some attention on account of their mechanical interest. These are clearly illustrated and described in the cut and specifications shown on adjoining page.

The working of the sostenuto pedal and of the new soft pedal device will be readily comprehended by reference to the cut.

It will be noted, in the first place, that the metallic action brackets which were omitted in the previous drawing for the sake of exhibiting the working parts more clearly, are now shown.

The "sostenuto pedal" is devised to permit the sustaining of a chord while the fingers of the performer, for the purpose of continuing the melody, are withdrawn from the keys. It will be observed that the action is provided with a rod (22) which is connected with a pedal and is adapted to be brought into contact with an additional damper-lever (23). This additional lever is provided with a tongue of felt, and when the rod is turned on its axis, this tongue engages with a similar metallic device on the rod, thus holding the damper up as long as the rod is kept in the position of contact. When the key is pressed down, the damper rises to clear the string, and brings the additional lever up with it, so that, if the rod is now caused to revolve, the tongues on each engage one with another and the damper is held up as long as the pedal is pressed down and irrespective of the position of the key. Provided that the keys are first depressed, the pedal will always hold up as many of the dampers as are thus raised. The result is to sustain the sound of the strings after the hand has been removed from the key. This gives a more permanent character to the harmonization of a melody, without the dissonance that comes from the releasing of all the dampers by the ordinary "*forte*" pedal. The "sostenuto pedal" is generally situated between the others in the lyre or pedal case at the level of the player's feet.

The second device is also most interesting. It consists of a method for softening the sound of the string, by a method similar to that which is employed in the upright. It is claimed, and with some justice, that the use of the shifting key-frame is attended with various complications, and that the motion tends to hinder the adjustment of the action to the strings. Moreover the hammers become unevenly worn by being continually caused to strike two, instead of three, strings and this operates to cause loss of directness in the hammer-strokes.

In this new device, the hammer is provided with a swing-rail (25), having a cushion for the hammer-rebound similar to the ordinary cushion that is supported upon the wippen in most actions, and a rod (26) for pivoting it to the metallic action frame (24). The swing-rail also is fitted with a lifter (27), which is operated by the soft pedal through a lifter-rod (28). So far the process is simple. The effect of the motion of the swing-rail is to bring the hammer closer to the string and to soften the tone. But this is only accomplished at the cost of lost motion between the capstan-screw and the key. To avoid the loss of touch thus brought about, the lifter-rod is connected with two compensating levers (29) and (30), which are so adjusted that they form a continuous link between the parts where the lost motion would occur, and thus preserve the continuity of touch and the weight that is lost by the different actuating positions of the hammer. The ingenuity of this device commends it to the student of pianoforte mechanism, and the makers are entitled to great praise for the successful achievement of this important modification.

We may conclude our survey by giving a list of the materials of which grand actions are constructed.

Various Woods—

Pear tree	Damper heads.
Holly	Jacks and other small parts.
Sycamore	Jacks and other small parts.
Ebony	Tops of black keys.
Maple	Hammer moldings and shanks.
Mahogany	Hammer moldings, buttons, etc.
White pine	Key-frames.

Felts and Cloths—

Baize	On key-frames, hammer-rails, etc.
Baize	Punchings.
Flannel cloth	Bushing centre pin holes, damper lifter holes, etc.
Tone felt	Upper and under felt for hammer.

Hard felt	Bass damper wedges.
Soft felt	Treble dampers, etc.
Flannel	Sundry action parts.

Leathers and Skins—

Doeskin	
Buckskin	Various parts of action, operating faces of hammer-butts, etc.
Elkskin	
Ivory	Tops of white keys.
Celluloid	Fronts of white keys.
Graphite	Lubrication of working parts.
Iron	Action frames, screws, etc.
Brass	Centre pins, springs, pedal-feet, etc.

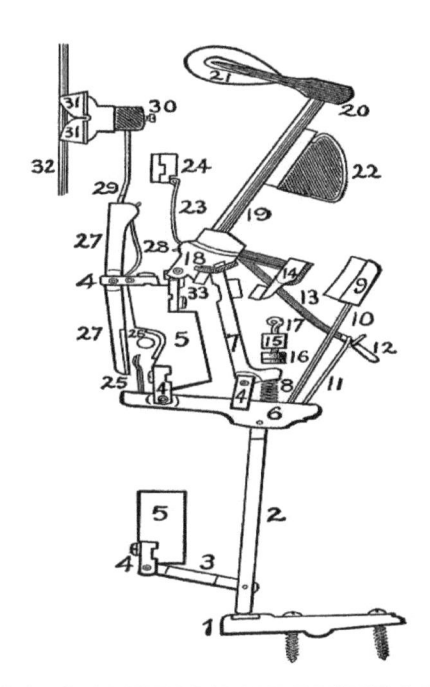

STANDARD AMERICAN UPRIGHT ACTION.

- 1. Key-rocker.
- 2. Abstract.
- 3. Abstract-lever.
- 4. Flange.
- 5. Action-rail.
- 6. Wippen.
- 7. Jack.
- 8. Jack-spring.
- 9. Check.
- 10. Check-wire.
- 11. Bridle-wire.
- 12. Tip of bridle-tape.
- 13. Bridle-tape.
- 14. Back-stop.
- 15. Regulating rail.
- 16. Regulating button.
- 17. Regulating screw.
- 18. Hammer-butt.
- 19. Hammer-shank.
- 20. Hammer-molding.
- 21. Hammer-head.
- 22. Hammer-rail.
- 23. Hammer-butt spring.
- 24. Hammer-spring rail.
- 25. Damper-spoon.
- 26. Damper-lifting rod.
- 27. Damper-lever.
- 28. Damper-lever spring.

- 29. Damper-wire.
- 30. Damper-block.
- 31. Damper-head.
- 32. String.
- 33. Continuous brass hammer-butt flange.

We are now able to turn our attention to the action mechanism of the upright pianoforte. The historical chapter of this work contains a short description of the early history of the upright form. Of course, it will at once be seen that the only real mechanical difficulty in designing a vertical type of pianoforte was to be found in the department of touch-mechanism. The problem was indeed primarily of the action. As such it is interesting to note the efforts of Hawkins, Southwell and Loud, to produce an action that would approach in efficiency that of the grand. It was Robert Wornum, however, who found the solution, though not until nearly the end of the first quarter of the nineteenth century. The principle applied by Wornum possessed such value that it has never been superseded, and remains today the distinguishing feature of the upright action.

We refer, of course, to the tape. As applied to the action of uprights, this device has become universal, and all upright actions in consequence have for years been everywhere similar as to general design. Thus we do not find those radical differences of actuating principle that to this day distinguish American from certain European grand pianofortes. This is partly due to the fact that the great battles had already been fought out when the first successful upright actions were made. At present, the only remaining types of the ancient "sticker" leather-hinged action are to be found in old-fashioned and obsolete European pianofortes of the cheaper grade. None are made now, however, except in the case of a very few worthless commercial English instruments. In the United States the "sticker" action has hardly been heard of.

Thus it seems unnecessary to give detailed drawings of any but the accepted type of upright action. The reader's attention is immediately called, therefore, to the drawing herewith given.

The method of operation may be seen very clearly. Depression of the key, to which is screwed the key-rocker (1), causes the Abstract (2) and the Wippen (6) to rise. This brings the Jack (7) to bear against the butt (18), which is raised, forcing the hammer (20) and (21) through the shank (19) against the string (32). As the hammer strikes, the rise of the jack has brought its tail against the regulating-button (16), which trips it up so that it falls towards the back-stop (14). The butt, being thus left free, drops back, assisted by the pull of the tape (13), until the back-stop is caught and held by the check (9), thus leaving time for the jack to get back under the hammer butt through the aid of the spring (8). Repetition of the hammer is thus assured, and while the rapidity of stroke cannot be so great as that of the grand, it is sufficiently so to satisfy ordinary users. Sometimes a spring is fastened to the front of the jack in connection with a silk loop and cord which stretches back and engages with the hammer spring (23). The latter is then fastened to the hammer butt instead of to a rail (24). This arrangement gives a far more rapid repetition to the action and causes it to approach the delicacy of the double escapement of the grand.

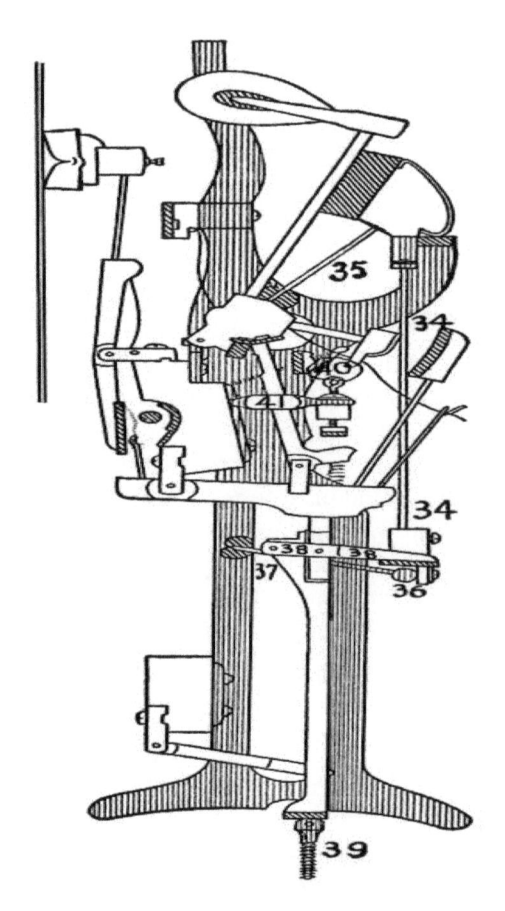

UPRIGHT ACTION SHOWING LOST-MOTION DEVICE, METALLIC REGULATING RAIL SUPPORT, CAPSTAN SCREW, JACK REGULATING RAIL AND METALLIC ACTION BRACKETS.

- 34. Hammer-rail lifter-wire.
- 35. Hammer-rail swing-lever.
- 36. Hammer-rail lifter rod.
- 37. Lifter-rod lever.
- 38. Compensation-lever.
- 39. Capstan-screw.
- 40. Rail for limiting return movement of jack.
- 41. Metallic regulating rail support.

The pedal mechanism is the same as in the grand. The "*piano*" effect is obtained by pushing forward the hammer-rail (22), so that the hammers approach nearer to the strings. The "*forte*" pedal effect is obtained by use of the damper lifting rod (26) which is turned rearwards and forces back the whole line of damper heads so that they leave the strings.

The lost motion that occurs in the action when the "*piano*" pedal is used has been overcome in a most ingenious manner, and by means similar to those already described in the discussion of the grand action. The trouble to be overcome is the same, namely the lifting up of the abstract from the rocker or capstan screw caused by the forcing of the hammers towards the strings. This causes loss of touch and is very irritating to the performer.

The drawing given herewith also shows the metallic action bracket for supporting the action and the capstan screw that is used as an alternate to the key-rocker.

The lost motion attachment operates through the rod (36) which lifts the hammer rail and at the same time brings into play the compensation lever (38), which takes up the space between the abstract and the key that would otherwise intervene. Thus the touch remains true irrespective of the position of the hammer.

The materials that are required for the manufacture of the upright action do not differ from those, which we have already classified as pertaining to the grand.

The adjustment of the upright action requires that the same precautions be taken in the measurement of the key-bed, of the height of the action between the keys and striking-point of hammers, the distance of hammer from strings when at rest and so on. All these assist the action maker to adjust the alignment of the hammers and the height of the abstracts. The size of the pianoforte sometimes requires the omission of the abstracts, in which case the bottom of the wippen is felted and brought into contact with the capstan or rocker direct. All these details are attended to by the action maker when the proper measurements are given. The marking on a stick of the run of the strings is done just as was suggested for the grand scale.

In conclusion, it may be mentioned that much similarity exists between certain parts of the action of both types of instrument. It has become customary to make the length of the hammer shank and hammer butt, when fitted together, about five inches, counting from the center pin of the butt to the middle of the hammer molding. This measurement will be found correct for both grands and uprights.

The length of the hammer blow is always as nearly as possible $1\ ^{24}/_{25}$ inches for the bass end, graduating to $1\ ^{9}/_{10}$ scant in the treble. These dimensions should be maintained at all costs. The key lengths that we gave before are applicable to all forms of uprights. When provided with these data the action maker will be able to put out a mechanism that will fulfill the individual requirements of each kind of instrument.

CHAPTER XIII.
REGULATION OF PIANOFORTE TOUCH MECHANISM.

We may presume that the reader is by this time quite familiar with the appearance and use of the various parts of the grand and upright pianoforte action, both as assembled and detached. We may therefore proceed to give general instructions for the adjustment of these within the instrument and the regulation of the various working parts into proper harmony with one another.

We say "general instructions" advisedly; for it is quite out of the question to teach action finishing and regulating by means of written directions. Experience and the practical routine of the shop must be gone through by anyone who hopes to be able to do this kind of work well. For there are few departments of mechanical endeavor that demand such skill, care, and patience as the regulation of pianoforte mechanism.

Nevertheless the directions that we shall give in this chapter will be sufficient to make him who reads and digests them a very efficient critic. It is much to the employer to be able to estimate correctly the value of each practical detail of the construction, and the correctness of the manner in which it is executed. This chapter is intended to provide as much of this knowledge as may be imparted by means of written words.

We shall begin with the grand action, following the method that has been pursued throughout this work.

The first step in the regulating and adjustment of the grand action is taken by the "action-finisher." He receives the action and keys separately. The former is without hammers or dampers and the latter without rockers or capstan screws. The action has to be placed within the space destined for it in the instrument and the proper position for it noted. If the action has been well made there should be no difficulty in seeing that it fits its place correctly. The action is screwed on to the key-frame through its metallic brackets and the capstan screws are put into the keys at the proper points so that they engage with the cushions on the bottom of the wippens. When this has been done the weight of the action upon any one of the keys should be noted and the action may then be removed. A piece of lead should then be taken and fastened to the back of each key. This lead must have the same weight as the action has upon each key. The keys will then remain in their proper positions when the action is removed, and the work of leveling them may then be begun. Remembering the depth of touch that was prescribed in the last chapter, let the extreme bass and treble keys be adjusted to an equivalent height by wooden blocks through their front rail pins. Then run a straight edge over the keys and proceed to adjust their levels by means of the thin paper punchings that are provided for the purpose. These come in various thicknesses and are laid over the balance rail pins and under the cloth punchings that must first have been placed in position both on the balance rail and the front rail. When the leveling is accomplished let the action be screwed on again. Then let the hammers be glued on. The striking point of the hammers must be carefully measured and the directions already given as to the striking of the highest hammer must be observed. It will be remembered that one-tenth of the string was recommended for the highest hammers, graduating down to the ideal one-ninth and one-eighth. The scale draughtsman will prepare a marking stick showing the true hammer line. The hammers are glued on absolutely at right angles to the plane of the strings. After they are dry, they must be adjusted to the proper position by the capstan screws or rockers. They must lie just over and not quite touching the wippen cushions. Let them also be aligned to each other, horizontally, with great exactness. Be sure that the keys work easily and that the depth of touch is roughly adjusted as already provided for.

It next becomes necessary to fix the damper mechanism. This is chiefly situated in the back of the action and the damper levers are to be so adjusted that they rest a little above the backs of the keys, ready to be engaged with them when the fronts of the keys are depressed. The dampers must fit on to the strings straight and must drop with sufficient force to effect an instantaneous damping. The damper levers are leaded for this purpose.

The instrument is then taken in hand by the action regulator. His work is most important. He first sees that the level of the keys is perfect and that they are properly balanced when suspended without the action. If any defects are found here they are remedied by changes in the leading. The keys should be so leaded that they balance when tested on a scale and the weight of touch with the action fitted must not be more than two and one-quarter ounces.

The alignment of the hammers is then corrected and the length of the hammer stroke, as laid down in Chapter XII, is adjusted by means of the capstan screw or rocker. The jack is so regulated by its button and screw that the trip up of the jack occurs when the hammer is $5/32$ of an inch from the string. The checks must catch the hammers when they have fallen three-quarters of an inch away from the strings. The tails of the hammer-moldings must be roughened and the checks be so slanted that the catch is sure and tight.

The escapement lever is then considered. The spring that governs it requires adjustment. It must be sufficiently strong to cause the hammer to dance and jump a little on the lever when the key is released. The escapement lever must also be regulated by means of the hook that is found at its rear end. There must be space enough between the hook and the lever to ensure that the catch of the hammer by the check is at all times free. The screw that regulates the rise of the escapement lever must also be attended to. It is necessary that the movement of the lever be arrested before the hammer has quite risen to the point of the trip up of the jack.

The after-touch under the front of the keys is regulated by means of paper punchings. If enough punchings are placed under the keys to make very hard pressure necessary to force a release of the hammer, then punchings of $\frac{1}{32}$ of an inch in thickness must be removed to make the after touch correct.

The keys must also be made to descend evenly as judged from the top. Unevenness is corrected also by the judicious use of punchings. In regulating the dampers there are many small details to be watched. The lifter-wires must work freely in the bushings and the heads must lie straight upon the strings. This is especially important as regards the bass wedge-dampers. There must be a small space between the damper levers and the felted backs of the keys and the rise of the damper heads when the levers are lifted must be even and facile. The height of ascent of the damper heads must not exceed one-fifth of an inch, and a little more when the whole of them are lifted by the pedal-rod. The sostenuto rod must also be adjusted so that the damper lever tongues are caught when the rod is revolved. Care must be taken that the rod does not catch the tongues when the pedal is not in use.

The pedal mechanism is simple. It is essential to see that the feet work in the lyre without scraping; hence lubrication with graphite and tallow is necessary. The rods that connect with the action levers must so engage as to be just in contact without bearing too much. The soft *"piano"* pedal must engage with the shifting lever so as to allow a small space between it and the point of contact with the key-frame. The strength of the reaction spring in the case must be arranged so that the key-board is pushed back with promptness upon the release of the pedal. The *"forte"* pedal must be adjusted so that its connecting rod is in contact with the damper lever lifting rail, but not enough to operate without the depression of the pedal. The sostenuto pedal requires to be arranged to revolve the sostenuto rod instantly. Here the rod has to be revolved its entire distance before it operates and the adjustment may therefore be made quite close.

These directions will enable one at least to be sure that the regulation of a grand pianoforte action has been properly done; although it is not to be expected that the innumerable small details of practical work are to be learned other than practically. It must especially be borne in mind that the use of tools and facility in handling them and making definite adjustments with them is a matter of long and patient practice. The above instructions are intended merely to set the routine method before the reader, so that he may approach the subject with a correct knowledge of principles.

The regulation and adjustment of the upright action is precisely similar as to principles. The differences occur through the somewhat dissimilar method whereby repetition is attained and the great variation in the general position of the parts with reference to the strings.

The action of the upright is fastened, by means of the metallic brackets, to iron bolts which are set up in the key-bed. The height of these bolts depends upon the dimensions of the instrument and the striking point of the strings. In setting the action in place great care must be exercised in seeing that the hammer line lies truly in regard to the run of the strings. Errors in the casting of the plate often lead to a distortion of the true string-line and the action finisher must take care to set the action with due regard to these matters. When the action, which is minus hammers and dampers, is thus set in, the keys may be placed under it for the purpose of marking the points where the capstan screws or rockers must be set. The hammers and dampers are then glued in and adjusted for position with regard to the strings. If the action and keys are truly proportioned, it is always possible to make the length of the key just as recommended in the last chapter. Sometimes the size of the pianoforte makes impossible the employment of capstans or rockers with abstracts. In this case it is customary either to use a dowel prop or to lay the wippen directly upon the key. When the dowel prop is used it is driven firmly into the key, and its upper end, which is a wooden rod into which the lower spike is screwed, impinges against the wippen. In laying the place for the dowel to be driven, it must be remembered that it is necessary for the head of the dowel to hit the bottom of the wippen squarely. But the dowel describes a curve at its head when the key is moving, and the wippen has to be provided with a felted foot, curved so as to accommodate this circular motion of the dowel. This motion must be observed carefully, so that the dowel does not lay too far forward or back of the wippen foot when the key is at either of its extreme positions. The regulation proper now begins.

Abstracts, or dowels, are always regulated by a screw. This is either in the form of a capstan or of a rocker, or of the movable part of the dowel itself. The adjustment must be made with reference to the position of the jack under the hammer butt. It is necessary that the jack be just in contact with the notched heel of the butt. After the hammers and dampers have been put in and their positions with reference to the keys adjusted, it becomes necessary to regulate the escape of the hammer by means of the regulating buttons and the jacks. The directions given for grands apply here. The hammer springs must be put in place and the fall of the hammers noted. If they stick, the bushings are too tight or some cognate trouble exists which can be easily remedied with a drop of oil on the affected part.

The checks must be adjusted to the back-stops and made to stand square to them and they must also be arranged to catch the back-stops when the hammer has recovered about two-thirds of an inch from the string. We know that the length of the hammer blow should be from $1\ ^{24}/_{25}$ of an inch in the bass to $1\ ^{9}/_{10}$ of an inch in the treble.

The tapes must be adjusted so that they begin to exercise their pull when the hammer is started away from the strings. They must not be strained too tight, but should be left just a little loose, so that when the soft pedal pushes the hammers towards the strings the abstracts or dowels do not at once leave the keys.

The dampers are adjusted, as to position, like those of the grand—that is, they must lie square on the strings and be in a straight line with one another. Their movements are directed by the spoons and these must be so bent that the damper begins to move when about one-third of the angular motion of the key has taken place. When actuated by the pedal, they must fall against the back of the hammer spring rail, which is felted for the purpose, and their motion must be instantaneous when the pedal is depressed. The pedal mechanism is concealed behind the bottom frame of the case and will be found to be precisely similar to that of the grand, except as regards the mounting and pivoting of the levers. These must be kept lubricated with graphite and tallow to prevent squeaking. The connection of the soft pedal with the hammer rail must be close so that instantaneous action results when the pedal is operated. The motion of the pedal may push the hammers one-half of their stroke length towards the strings, not more.

The leveling of the keys and the regulation of touch have already been described; nothing further need be said except that these operations are more easily performed in the upright owing to the open way in which everything is set in.

It is unnecessary to go further into detail in regard to the regulation of actions. Enough has been said to lay bare the general principles, and, as was stated before, the rest comes from experience only. A text-book can never replace an apprenticeship, but we cannot deny its value in laying down correct principles for the man who wants to know how things should be done.

As a fitting conclusion to the present discussion, we may now note the order of the various processes which combine to make up the manufacture of a pianoforte, from the cutting of the lumber to the final tuning in the wareroom.

The various kinds of lumber that are to be used are exposed, after cutting and rough dressing, in a lumber-yard. Here they remain from three to ten years according to the kind of wood and the degree of care that is taken by the manufacturer. The best makers take the greatest care in seasoning their lumber.

The first operations to be considered are those of the saw-mill. Here the rough work for the case-making is done, and the moldings for actions and cases are turned out. The rough cases are then sent to the case department and made up into shape. The bent rims are there glued together for the grands, and the sides and frames of the uprights are shaped. The back framing, wrest-planks and other parts of the case and back construction are also put together in the case department.

In the meantime, the machine work has gone in the rough from the saw-mill to the "action department," where it is cut, shaped and made up into the delicate action parts. These have to be leathered, felted, provided with brackets, springs and the other accessories and assembled. The hammers are covered, dampers, prepared, and the whole of the action work is thus made ready against the time when the case shall be in condition to receive it. This action and hammer work is generally done by specialists, who supply many different makers with actions according to their particular scales and patterns.

Meanwhile the cases have been sent to the varnish room and are here prepared with filler and stain to receive the varnish finish. The best instruments have their cases left about four months in the varnish room, receiving eight or ten coats at intervals of ten days or more.

While this is going on, the sound-board department is occupied in preparing the sheets of spruce for manufacture into sound-boards. Here great care and skill are necessary to obtain the proper gradation of thickness at all parts of the board's surface. When the boards are finished, they are put into drying rooms, to remain until wanted for ribbing, bridging and insertion within the instruments.

The first operation in the assembling of the parts is performed by the "bellyman." He takes the sound-board, ribs it and affixes the bridges according to pattern, bores the tuning pin holes in the wrest-plank, and fastens on the iron plate, which was cast to pattern in the iron foundry, to the back, upon which the completed sound-board has by this time been glued.

Then the "stringer" receives the bellied back, puts on the strings and pressure bar (if the latter is used instead of agraffes). The first rough approximation to pitch is then made by the "chipper," who pulls the strings up roughly two or three times in succession at intervals of about twenty-four hours.

The case is then turned over to the "side-gluer," if the instrument be an upright. The case of the grand is incorporated with the back and is put together before the bellying. The side-gluer affixes the sides and key-bed of the upright and also the bottom-board, which contains the trap-work for the pedal mechanism. If the instrument be a grand this department confines itself to the fitting and adjustment of the lyre. After the sides are thus affixed the case is returned to the "flowing-room," where the final coat of "flowing" varnish is carefully applied. This requires ten days to dry hard.

The case is now ready for the "action finisher." His work of setting in the action and keys and putting the instrument into rough playing condition has been described in detail.

The pianoforte is then given its first rough tuning by the "rough-tuner," who surrenders it in turn to the "fly-finisher." In this department the top and bottom frames, fall-board, panels, key-blocks, name-board, key-slip, hinges, music desk and other parts of the cabinet work are adjusted and fitted. After fitting they are removed from the case and sent to the "polishing department" to be made ready for the final setting up.

The next operation is performed by the "action regulator." His work, which includes the finishing touches to the adjustments made by the action-finisher and side-gluer, has already been gone over in detail.

The instrument is by this time ready for another and somewhat more careful tuning. Here appears the "second tuner." The instrument then is permitted to remain in its existing condition until two more tunings have been given at intervals of a week.

The "fine-regulator" next takes the instrument and proceeds to review the work of the action-regulator and correct any deficiencies in touch or repetition that may have been effected by the pounding of the rough tuners.

The "tone-regulator" is next called upon, and his delicate work is needed to give to the pianoforte evenness of tone throughout and an agreeable quality.

Then the polishers rub down the sides, the smaller parts being already polished as noted before, and give to the instrument its glossy and mirror-like finish. The "setter-up" then puts the various cabinet work parts together and the "fine-tuner" gives the final tuning. Lastly, the superintendent looks over the whole work, and woe betide the unlucky wight who has slurred or skimped his part.

The details listed above are, of course, subject to variations in the order in which they are performed. The variations are according to the practice of individual shops. Of course, it may at any time be required to give more tunings, especially if the pianoforte is left on the floor of the factory very long. But there should never be less than four or five.

When the instrument is sent to the wareroom or shipped to the dealer extra tunings are given according to the caprice or knowledge of both.

CHAPTER XIV.
TUNING AND TONE REGULATION OF THE PIANOFORTE.

The art of tuning the pianoforte is one of considerable complexity and obscurity. During all the time that has elapsed since the key-board instrument first came into being, controversies innumerable have raged over the multifarious questions that the practice of the art implies. This distressing state of affairs is primarily due to the fact that a system of "tempering" the sounds produced by key-board instruments is necessary, in order that playing in more than one key may be possible.

The whole matter of musical intonation was treated with some completeness in the early part of this work, and the reader may be expected to comprehend the principles of the Equal Temperament upon which the tuning of the pianoforte and of all other fixed tone instruments is now universally based. It is not within our province, in the course of a treatise upon the principles of pianoforte construction, to venture too deeply into the quagmires that surround the aspirant for the honors of the tuner. The discussion of musical intonation and the Equal Temperament was made for the principal purpose of acquainting the student with the reason for the peculiar construction of scales, as to their string lengths, and to make clear the *raison d'etre* of the frequent divergences from theoretical proportions of strings and tones that we have been obliged to note.

The scale designer is better equipped for his task, however, if he possess a working knowledge of the principles upon which the science and art of tuning are based. This is the justification for the space and time devoted to the exhibition of certain of these principles in the earlier portion of this book. As a further contribution to this useful body of knowledge, we shall point out here the general scheme whereby the tuner proceeds to the execution of his important, indeed essential, portion of the whole work.

The practical work of tuning is performed by the aid of certain acoustical phenomena which enable the tuner to distinguish between sounds that are very nearly in unison. As the Equal Temperament requires the slight roughening of all the intervals with the exception of the unison and octave, it is clear that there is great value in a method of estimating, not only the unisonal or non-unisonal condition of two sounds, but also the exact amount of difference that may occur between them. The phenomena mentioned are called "beats," and it is well that their physical basis should be described here.

From what has been said before, it is clear that musical sounds, generated as they are by the periodic agitation of the air according to fixed laws, are but the audible manifestations of a peculiar form of air-motion. The particular form of air-motion can best be described as a wave. Whenever a sonorous body is excited into vibration it causes the surrounding atmosphere to make motions that correspond to its own. A vibrating body such as we have described (together with the segments thereof) partakes of a motion that may be compared to that of a pendulum. There is a rhythmic swinging back and forth of the body and its segments, with the result that the immediately adjacent layers of air are excited into alternate states of compression and expansion; or, more correctly, of condensation and rarefaction. This rhythmic motion is imparted by the layers of air adjacent to the sonorous body to the next adjacent layers, and so on. The result of this is that a wave is formed, the length of which varies inversely as the number of vibrations performed by the sonorous body. This wave is called a sonorous wave.

Now we know that sounds are at the same pitch when they are generated by sonorous bodies having the same speed of vibration, and it is easy to perceive that, if two such bodies are sounding together, the condensations and rarefactions of the layers of air will synchronize with each other, so that both will be exciting condensations at the same instant and likewise will generate rarefactions simultaneously. And even if the two bodies have not exactly the same speed, the result will be equally simple as long as their speeds bear simple ratios to each other. Thus two bodies which are emitting sounds at the interval of an octave or of a fifth or fourth will generate condensations and rarefactions in such a manner that they will not interfere one with another. But the case is different where two sounds are separated by differences in pitch that cannot be expressed by simple ratios. For example, if one sound be one vibration per second higher than another, it is clear that by the time that the first sounding body has completed its given number of vibrations in one second, the other will be one vibration behind. When, therefore, the vibrations of the first body are continued into the next second the condensation of one wave will be completely synchronous with neither the condensation nor the rarefaction of the other. The obvious result is that at a certain point the condensations of each wave concur while at another point the condensation of one crosses the rarefaction of the other. In the first case we have a considerable augmentation of sound and in the other case a complete silence. As the waves thus approach and recede there is a gradual diminution of sound followed by a complete cessation for a small fraction of a second, and then a gradual increase until the point of greatest augmentation occurs. This latter happens when the two condensations concur, and the gradual rise and fall of the sound correspond to the gradual approach of this concurrence in the first case and to the similar advance of the point of crossing in the second. This phenomenon of alternate augmentation and diminution of sound separated by an almost inappreciable interval of silence occurs whenever two sounds of nearly the same pitch are heard simultaneously. These peculiar changes in the intensity of a sound are denominated "beats."

This description of the physical nature of "beats" will be sufficient to make clear to us how a recognition of them is of value to the tuner. From what we have just said, it will be observed that the number of beats that may be set up between any two sounds depends upon the difference in the frequency of the two sonorous bodies. So that the number of beats form a true guide to the exact amount of difference between sounds that are nearly in consonance. Thus, if it becomes a matter of tuning a certain interval a little flat or sharp, in order to comply with the requirements of Equal Temperament, the operation may be readily performed by observing the number of beats that are heard between the two sounds when one of them is sharpened or flattened. So that all schemes of tuning must necessarily be founded upon a recognition of this important phenomenon.

At this point it will be well to reiterate the fact that the Equal Temperament owes its popularity and long prevalence to the wonderful facility of modulation which it possesses. While it certainly involves discords and disharmonics that the mesotonic system, for instance, avoided, yet the fact that it does not limit the expression of musical ideas to a few scales, but permits the composer to roam at will through the whole field of tonalities, has given to it a deeply founded popularity that has not yet been seriously challenged. We must bear in mind that the Equal Temperament is the first fact, the "prius," the "proton hemin," as it were, of musical performance. Obviously, therefore, the importance of a proper and close adherence to this system in the tuning of fixed-tone instruments cannot be insisted upon too strongly. The reader has already had occasion to examine a comparative table which showed the pitches of a true and of a corresponding tempered scale. He will have noted that the tempered scale errs very greatly in respect to certain intervals. The task of equalizing the thirteen sounds which a fixed-tone instrument allows to the octave, involves in each interval a greater or less divergence from purity, according to the ratio of such interval. Thus we find that the error of a tempered third is greater than that of a fifth, and so on. Now, if the four minor thirds within the compass of an octave be considered, it will be found that the octave to the tonic which is produced from the last of these is a good deal sharper than the octave taken direct from the tonic. Again the octave produced from the building up of the three major thirds within the same compass is very much flatter than the octave taken direct from the tonic. Again, it will be remembered that there are twelve fifths within the compass of seven octaves. The last sound in this progression of fifths is considerably sharper than the sound that is produced by taking a series of seven octaves from the tonic. Without going into figures, we may give the differences thus noted concisely as follows:

In the cases above considered the octaves obtained by building up intervals differ from the straight octave in the following proportions:

- The octave produced from minor thirds is sharper in the ratio 1296:1250.
- The octave produced from major thirds is flatter in the ratio 125:128.
- The octave produced from fifths is sharper in the ratio 531441:524288.

Obviously, therefore, it will be necessary to tune all the minor thirds, within an octave, flat by one-fourth each of the ratio given for them. It will also be necessary to tune each of the major thirds sharp by one-third of the ratio proper to those intervals. Likewise each of the perfect fifths must be made flat by one-twelfth of the ratio given above for fifths.

We are thus able to understand just how great divergencies from purity are involved in the Equal Temperament of major thirds, minor thirds and fifths. As far as the other intervals are concerned, it is obvious that if the thirds and fifths are equally tempered and the octaves tuned quite purely, the other intervals will be subjected simultaneously and automatically to a similar process of temper.

Now from what we learned of the phenomena of beats, we must conclude that the tempering process when applied to these intervals will generate beats between the sounds that compose each interval. We know that beats must occur when the sounds that form any consonant interval are not quite in tune with one another. We also know that the frequency of the beats depends upon the difference in frequency of the generating sounds. We can, therefore, easily see that those intervals that are subjected to the greatest amount of tempering will produce the greatest number of beats. And further, as the actual frequencies of the sounds increase according to their pitch, it is equally obvious that the tempering will result in greater differences as to actual frequency between the true and the corresponding tempered intervals. Therefore the number of beats that any tempered interval generates varies directly as the pitch of the sounds that form the interval. The higher the pitch, the greater the number of beats. Conversely, the lower the pitch, the smaller the number of beats.

Now we have already noted that the phenomena of beats afford an absolutely precise test for the consonance or otherwise of an interval. If we can estimate the number of beats that should occur between the sounds of any given equally tempered interval, we can always tune such an interval in the Equal

Temperament by noting the number of beats and adjusting this to the theoretical number in the calculations. It is not possible accurately to follow the number of beats that are supposed to be between any given intervals in Equal Temperament even when the pitch of the tonic of the interval that is being tuned is precisely similar to the corresponding sound in the calculations. It is not possible, therefore, in practice, to tune with such accuracy as theory would demand, but an approximation may be obtained. If we could secure an absolute standardization of pitch for the pianoforte it would be possible to construct tables that would show the exact number of beats that ought to occur between all the equally tempered sounds within the whole compass. In default of such a method, it is necessary to resort to a variety of tests and to prove the correctness of the tempering of each interval by comparison of the different intervals of various kinds that to which each sound, as it is completed, gives rise. If, for example, we find that any given sound, when tuned, gives the same number of beats with the tenth below as it does with the third below, which is one octave above the tenth, then we have some assurance that the sound in question is properly tempered. If this assurance is confirmed by a complete absence of beats between the given sound and its octave, above or below, then we have an almost absolute assurance as to the correctness of the work.

It is then upon the phenomena of beats that the tuner depends for a guide to the correctness of the work in which he is engaged. By noting the frequency of the beats at some places, or their absence at others, he is able to judge most accurately whether any interval is tuned too sharp or too flat, or whether any octave is tuned purely or the reverse. All good tuning depends entirely upon such estimation of the beats, and the greatest difficulty that the tuner encounters lies in the fact that he must try to equalize the frequencies of the beats between all the intervals of the same kind within the compass of each octave. If this work is well and truly done it properly deserves the name of art, and, indeed, fine tuning is a fine art, one to be acquired by the painful and slow processes of manual practice and mental application. He who overcomes all obstacles to success and masters thoroughly the principles and practice of tuning is an artist in the truest sense.

In applying these principles to the tuning of the pianoforte, the problem that confronts us is to devise a rapid and simple means of tempering each sound within the seven odd octaves of the instrument, and to do this in such a manner that the deviation from purity shall be the same for all similar intervals within the compass of each octave.

Now it follows, from what has gone before, that the tempering of each separate interval, by itself, and without reference to any other, would be a very tedious and inaccurate process. It would, in fact, be quite impracticable to employ such means for intervals that require relatively large deviations from purity, especially in the higher pitched registers. There is, however, a method that largely obviates these difficulties. The middle octave of the instrument, which runs from F below middle C to F above it, is chosen, and the intervals within this octave are so tuned that the thirteen semitones which it contains become equally tempered sounds. The sounds within the next octave above or below are thereupon tuned from the former, each to its octave above or below, and this process is continued until all the sounds upon the key-board have been tuned.

It is easy to see that such a method possesses many and great advantages. All the difficult tempering of intervals that require large deviations from purity is confined to that portion of the piano where beats are most easily estimated; while the rest of the instrument is tuned by means of octave intervals, in which the test of purity is absence of beats, rather than the estimation of any number of them.

The tempering of the intervals in the middle octave is called "laying the bearings" and is the most difficult, as it is the most important, of the various processes incident to the practice of pianoforte tuning. The "accumulation of insensible into almost intolerable errors," as Mr. Ellis aptly terms it, continually besets the path of the tuner, especially if his preliminary knowledge be imperfect. The true estimation of beats, as generated by various intervals, is an art that is but slowly and painfully acquired, by long practice and training of the ear.

Examination of the pianoforte key-board shows us thirteen sounds within the compass of an octave. In proceeding to the conversion of these into equally tempered sounds, we have more than one method presented to us. We shall, of course, choose the octave which, as stated above, runs from F below middle C to F above it, and shall use, for our purposes, such adjacent sounds as we may consider necessary.

It is usual to take from a tuning-fork the pitch of the sound from which the tuning is begun. These instruments are tuned either to C, or A next above middle C. It is usual, in this country, to tune from C, and we shall, therefore, adopt that method.

Now there are various ways of setting about the "laying of the bearings." Some tuners work by thirds, others by fourths and fifths; others again use a series or circle of fifths joined by octaves. Whatever intervals are tuned, the idea is to include all the thirteen sounds within the octave and to use, as far as possible, only one or two kinds of intervals.

Of all these methods, the shortest, easiest and most accurate is that which employs fourths and fifths only. It is used in such a manner that, by tuning a circle of fifths and fourths, the last sound tuned provides the octave to the first, thus completing the circle and the octave of tempered sounds.

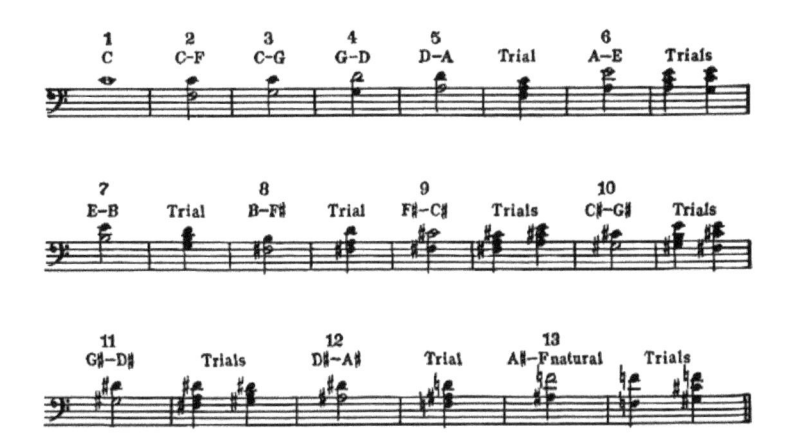

In this method we proceed as follows:

1. Pitch C is tuned by the tuning fork.
2. F below pitch C is tuned, being a tempered fifth.
3. G below pitch C is tuned, being a tempered fourth.
4. D above G is tuned, being a tempered fifth.
5. A below D is tuned, being a tempered fourth.
6. E above A is tuned, being a tempered fifth.
7. B below E is tuned, being a tempered fourth.
8. F sharp below B is tuned, being a tempered fourth.
9. C sharp above F sharp is tuned, being a tempered fifth.
10. G sharp below C sharp is tuned, being a tempered fourth.
11. D sharp above G sharp is tuned, being a tempered fifth.
12. A sharp below D sharp is tuned, being a tempered fourth.
13. F above A sharp is tuned, being a tempered fourth.

This last F is the octave to the first F tuned, and should coincide exactly with the latter.

The reader will, of course, realize that the tempering of these various intervals must be tested by means of the generated beats. Helmholtz, in "Die Lehre der Tonempfindungen," calculates that the tempered fifths should average .6 of a beat per second at standard pitch within the octave that we are treating. This is equivalent to three beats in five seconds. But it is impracticable to measure the generated beats upon the pianoforte in this manner. The tone of the instrument is too evanescent and fleeting. We may, however, attain to a very fair approximation. If, for example, each fifth be tuned so that two distinct beats are heard before the sound dies away, it will be found that the beat-rate is a near approximation to the calculated average. The two beats that we speak of occur in about three seconds, while the Helmholtz rate is three and one-third seconds for two beats.

Again Helmholtz gives an average beat-rate for tempered fourths in the same octave; namely, one per second. If we tune the fourths so that we hear three distinct beats we shall likewise obtain a very fair approximation to the calculated beat-rate.

We showed above that the last sound produced by the building up of a progression of twelve fifths is sharper than the sound produced by the piling up of seven octaves from the same tonic. The two sounds thus produced ought to coincide, for the compass of twelve fifths and of seven octaves is the same. We concluded, therefore, that the Equal Temperament required the flattening of all the fifths.

The meaning of the discussion is, therefore, that the fifths within the octave where the "bearings" are being laid must each be tuned flat by two beats. Or, rather, that the higher sound of every fifth must be flatter by two beats than if it were in consonance with the lower sound.

Again, if we tune the F below middle C two beats sharp of the latter (which is equivalent to tuning the fixed pitch sound C two beats flat of F) we shall obtain a properly tempered fifth. Now, if the octave above this F be taken it will be found to form a sharp fourth with middle C. For example, if the pitch of middle C be 264, then the pitch of F below it, in pure intonation, is two-thirds or 176. Assuming that the F be then tempered so as to be sharp by two vibrations, it will have a frequency of 178. The octave to this is 356 But this latter is a fourth above C 264 and should, therefore, be 352 Consequently we see that the fourths in Equal Temperament are to be tuned sharp ascending, or conversely, flat descending. As already explained, the beat-rate in the "bearings" should be nearly one per second or three beats, while the sound of the interval remains audible.

When the deviations from purity are as slight as in the cases that we have been considering, it is by no means easy to determine, at all times, whether the note that is being tuned is sharp or flat of its tonic. For the beats occur similarly in either case and few ears can determine the relative sharping or flatting without some extraneous aid. Fortunately, however, we have a variety of tests open to us, which for completeness and accuracy leave nothing to be desired.

To take a concrete example, during the "laying of the bearings" we first tune the F below middle C, then the G below middle C, and then the D above G. When we reach this last note, we find that a sixth has been obtained; namely, F—D. Now if the notes already tuned have been tempered, so as to be too *flat*, the resultant sixth will beat too *slowly*, and, conversely, if the tuned notes be too *sharp* the sixth will beat too *fast*.

This test may be amplified when we proceed to the next interval, D—A. When this latter note has been tuned, we have the triad F—A—C. F—A is a major third, and by referring to previous calculation we see that as such it must, when properly tempered, be considerably sharp. By noting the beats of the major third and likewise the beats of the sixth we may correct the tuning of all the sounds with which we have hitherto dealt. The same process is, of course, carried on throughout the whole process of "laying the bearings." The major thirds and sixths are tested continually as the tuning proceeds, and thus is provided a sure guide to the correctness of the fourths and fifths.

The correct beat-rates for the major thirds may be stated as about eight per second, while that for the major sixths is approximately eleven in the same period. Of course, as already stated, these rates per second cannot be measured with accuracy, but with practice one soon discovers by ear the proper roughness in each case, and is thus enabled to estimate the beat rates without much trouble. Every opportunity of examining the work of good tuners should be taken by the observer, who should note carefully the beat-rates which they assign to each kind of interval. In this way he will provide himself with practical examples of tempering of intervals which will be of great value to him.

Having thus determined the proper beat-rates for each of the intervals that are used in the "laying of the bearings," we may proceed to the further consideration of that convenient method for tuning the middle octave that has already been demonstrated.

In order to facilitate comprehension of the argument, the following table is given, showing graphically the sounds that are tuned in laying the bearings and the tests and trial chords—

The white notes are those to be tuned. The black notes are those already tuned.

The kind of deviation from purity of interval and the beat-rates are as follows:

- Upper notes of fifths must be tuned flat so as to give two distinct beats.
- Lower notes of fourths must be tuned flat so as to give three distinct beats.
- Upper notes of major thirds must be sharp so as to give approximately eight beats per second.
- Upper notes of major sixths must be sharp so as to give approximately eleven beats per second.

If the laying of the bearings has been accurately performed, the chords that are produced by the combination of the various sounds will be found to have very nearly the same roughness and to generate approximately the same number of beats. The best work is that which most closely approaches this standard.

After the bearings have thus been laid, it is necessary to continue the tuning of the instrument above and below the octave already treated. Now, since the octave to any given sound has exactly double the frequency of the former, and since octaves are to be tuned purely, it follows that we need only tune the remainder of the instrument by octaves up and down from the "bearings." The consonance of an octave is determined by the absence of beats, and, consequently, we have only to follow this rule to reproduce, in all parts of the piano, deviations from purity *relatively* the same as those which we have been at such pains to secure.

Of course, the *actual* number of beats in any given interval varies as the frequencies, and, consequently, the frequency of the beats increases regularly in the higher registers, while it similarly decreases in the lower portions. Thus the deviations from purity become much greater in the higher portions of the compass and incorrect laying of the bearings is, therefore, productive of more and more disagreeable results as the scale ascends. On the contrary, in the lower register these inaccuracies are less productive of irritation, as the frequencies of the beats become continually less.

Such, then, is the process of tuning the pianoforte in Equal Temperament. We have made no attempt to go into those practical details that are concerned with the ear-training, the manipulation of the hammer, or other cognate matters. These are entirely "*ex provincia*" of this work.

Nevertheless the person who digests the foregoing statement of the laws and methods of the art will be well equipped to pass upon the correctness of tuning, and this is sufficient for our purpose.

The work of tone-regulation opens up varying but not entirely dissimilar fields of research. The material of which the pianoforte hammer is constructed has an important influence upon the coloring of the sound that it draws from the string. In order that the influence of the pianoforte hammer in tone-coloring may be understood clearly, we shall investigate the matter with some completeness.

We have already investigated the compound nature of the sounds excited by the pianoforte strings. We know that the nature of these sounds varies as the method of excitement and as the nature of the resonance apparatus that surrounds the strings. Now the pianoforte strings are excited by being struck, and we have already noted that the point of striking must be carefully chosen. Further, we know that the amount of metal framing, the manner of adjusting the bridges, the nature of the sound-board and innumerable other details must be taken into consideration.

But by the time that the pianoforte comes into the hands of the tone-regulator, it is out of his power to affect the construction in any fundamental points. He is able to change only two things. These are the striking point and the condition of the hammer-heads. Even the former cannot be changed to any great extent. In the highest treble, however, it often becomes necessary to bend the hammer-shanks slightly in order that a more correct striking point may be obtained. But this must be done with great discretion and caution.

The object of tone-regulation is to ensure an agreeable tone and perfect evenness of quality throughout.

Obviously, this is so intimately bound up with the whole construction that it may be said that the tone-regulation begins with the drawing of the scale and is never finished until the pianoforte itself is completed. This would be a perfectly proper statement, but we have here to consider the final touches, as it were, that the tone-regulator may give to the tonal equipment.

When the instrument comes into his hands the hammers are still covered with the hard outer skin of the felt head. This must be removed with a sand-paper file. It then is necessary to sound each tone slowly and carefully, first loudly, and then less so. It will be found that some of the hammers produce a harsh and disagreeable timbre, while others may be too soft and mushy. Under all circumstances it is far better to endow the instrument, as far as is possible, with a quality that shall be comparatively mellow and round. Brilliancy cannot be forced artificially without spoiling the whole quality and imparting a thinness and roughness that is most disagreeable.

If the hammers are too hard at the crown, they have the acoustical effect upon the strings of exciting the upper dissonant partials to undue prominence. This occurs from the fact that when the head is hard it rebounds instantly from the string, and thus does not damp any of the dissonant partials. On the other hand, if the head be soft, the felt clings for a fraction of a second longer to the strings and effects the damping to a greater or less degree, according to the relative softness or hardness of the head.

It is thus possible, by discreet manipulation of the felt, to influence the character of the sounds to no small degree. The method is to pick up the felt, when it is to be softened, with a set of felt needles mounted in a handle for the purpose. It is essential to note whether the sound is the same when the hammer strikes with great force as it is when it strikes gently. If, for example, a gentle pressure on the key gives an agreeable quality, but harder strokes on the key destroy this, then we see that the crown of the hammer head is soft enough, but the felt cushion underneath is too hard. Fine needles are, therefore, employed to dig into the lower cushion of felt, while disturbing the consistency of the upper crown as little as possible. On the other hand, when the quality of sound is hard under all conditions, the upper surface of the hammer-head must be treated by picking it with heavier needles. Hardening of the felt may also be undertaken by covering the hammer-head with a damp cloth and then applying a hot iron.

The whole work is primarily one of practice and experience. No directions can do more than give an outline of the processes and the physical reasons for them. It is well, however, to lay down the laws that underly these processes, in order that practice may be supplemented and improved with theory.

CHAPTER XV.
THE DRAUGHTING OF THE PIANOFORTE SCALE.

Although, for obvious reasons, we speak of it thus late, yet it is true that the first and most important step in the designing of a pianoforte is the draughting of the scale. This process includes a complete planning of the iron plate and of the bridges, in fact of the whole arrangements for stretching the strings and maintaining their tension. This plan must indicate very clearly the exact length both of the vibratory portion and of the waste ends of each string; it must show the place on each string where the stroke of the hammer is to be directed, while the exact positions of each tuning-pin and hitch-pin must be laid down with equal certitude. Further, the place of the belly-bridges, their dimensions and manner of pinning, have to be shown on the drawing. Lastly, the fastening of the iron plate by screws and bolts must be indicated; together with the precise position of each individual screw, bolt and pin.

When this plan is in all respects complete, it has to be transferred to a wooden pattern. The inevitable shrinkage of paper always makes the retention of the proper measurements a matter of difficulty. This may be overcome by making the first drawing upon a sheet of wood, varnished to give a clear surface. If the drawing be made with India ink instead of with pencil, we shall have a complete and permanent record obtained in a superior manner.

When the wooden templet is to be made from such a drawing, it will not be found that there has been the shrinking or swelling caused by the use of paper, and the first drawing, if made after the method described, may be laid aside for any length of time.

Let us suppose that it is desired to draught the scale of an upright pianoforte. Having selected the size of pianoforte that is to be designed and the wooden "table" which is to serve for the drawing surface, we proceed as follows:

First lay down the line whereon all the hammers are to strike the strings. From this line as base we plot out the string lengths and the direction in which each runs; also the distance of each group from the immediately adjacent groups.

Having laid down the striking point line, we next proceed to indicate upon it, by suitable lines, the middle string of each three-string group. For the two-string groups a line is taken in the middle of the two strings. We call these lines "running lines." Then the string dimensions must be taken into consideration and calculated according to the rules laid down already. The highest treble strings run at right angles to the striking point line, and the running lines indicating the positions of the groups are to be placed accordingly. The distance between the running lines should be a shade more than one-half of an inch at the highest portions of the scale. It is found necessary to draw the running lines with increasing obliquity as their length increases, until at the end of the treble sections they are running at an angle of about 110 degrees counting from the treble end or 70 degrees counting from the bass end of the striking point line.

The lengths of the strings as determined by previous calculations mark the line of the belly-bridge. The bars that are to be cast in the plate must be allowed for in plotting the string plan. It is usual to place one of these at about F_2 and another at C, where the over-stringing customarily begins. The variations of individual scales and the requirements of particular sizes of instruments sometimes cause changes in this regard. This is one of the points that the designer must decide for himself.

The space between the running lines increases gradually as the length of them, on account of their oblique direction and the necessity for providing sufficient space for the dampers and hammers. The actual length of the strings as calculated must be laid down with reference to the striking point line. As has been pointed out, it is found better in practice to have the hammers strike the very high strings a little above the theoretical place. A good average would contemplate one-tenth of the length for the six highest strings, graduating down to one-ninth for the rest of the highest octave and the next below it. Before the lowest string of this last-named octave (C_3) is reached, the striking point is gradually lowered and two or three strings below C_3 it becomes one-eighth.

If we follow out this scheme we obtain the place where the scale rib intervenes at the pressure bar by taking one-tenth, one-ninth or one-eighth, as the case may be, of the length of each string. The remaining fraction of the length represents the correct distance between the striking point line and the nearest pin on the belly-bridge. Thus the belly-bridge and pressure bar lines are automatically formed as we go along.

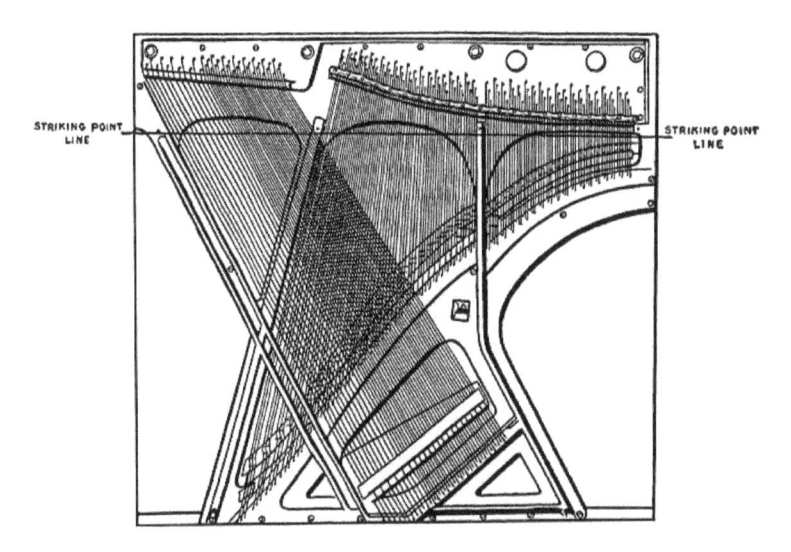

METHOD OF PLOTTING STRING PLAN BY MEANS OF STRIKING POINT LINE AND RUNNING LINES.

The sketch is intended merely as a general guide to the method outlined above, and only a few of the running lines are shown. The dark lines show the direction and position of the bars.

When the scale rib and pressure bar line has been obtained, it is necessary to make provision for the tuning pins, and particular care must be taken that the strings shall not rub against each other owing to incorrect placing of the pins.

When the drawing has thus been completed, we may take up the design of the iron plate. It will be remembered that we calculated a compensation factor for the shrinkage. This factor is $51/50$, and all dimensions where shrinkage may have effect must be multiplied by this amount.

Such dimensions are those of the height and width of the plate. Hence the lengths of the bars, the distances between them, and the positions of the bolts and screws as well as the string lengths must all be modified according to the shrinkage factor.

The wooden templet may be taken directly from the wooden table drawing by filling in the outlines and details of the iron plate on the latter and then copying these on to the templet subject to the shrinkage modifications required. It is well to regard one top side and also that at the treble as immovable, and to consider the shrinkage as coming from the bottom to the top and from the bass to the treble.

When the dimensions of the proposed plate are thus laid out on the surface of the templet, the bars, screw-sockets and bolt holes must be copied in wood and laid on the templet in the exact places that they will occupy in the finished plate. Thus we gradually evolve a complete wooden model of the iron plate, so that the iron founders may readily obtain a correct casting.

When the first casting comes back from the foundry, it should be carefully punched for the tuning-pin, bolt and screw holes. The first casting must be considered in reference to the fact that it represents only one shrinkage.

After the second casting is made from the first, the correctness of the calculations may be judged. But not until the first pianoforte is turned out according to the new scale can the designer find out how well his efforts have been rewarded.

Of course, the foregoing directions are but outlines of the method. The true inwardness of scale draughting cannot be explained here, or, indeed, otherwise than by practical experience. A certain facility in mechanical draughtsmanship is essential, and also close attention to the methods that have been laid down in regard to striking points, number of covered strings, number and place of bars, compensation for shrinkage, and the various other points that have been mentioned.

For the convenience of the plate-finisher, wooden patterns are provided, showing the position of hitch-pins, tuning-pin holes, screw-holes and bolt holes, corrected for shrinkage.

The belly-man must have patterns for the position of the bridges and for the bridge-pin boring. A wooden pattern is also required for the pressure bar.

When these details are completed, the draughtsman must possess himself in patience until his completed instrument is turned out.

If the rules so carefully demonstrated throughout this treatise are fully digested, the designer will be far on the way towards correct scale draughting. His native cunning, however, must be relied upon to carry him through when written directions fail.

CHAPTER XVI.
CONCLUSION.

If the present treatise has convinced the reader that the making of pianofortes is a very serious matter, and one not to be attacked in a spirit of levity, then one of its immediate objects has been attained.

Indeed there has been an abiding fear in the breast of the author that he might presently be charged with piling on the agony too strongly and searching with excessive zeal for scientific causes and rules when the shortest solutions may be found by empirical methods. This is not really the case, however, for the whole problem of the construction of pianofortes is naturally acoustical. While it is doubtless true that many pianofortes have been and are continually made, not merely with indifference to, but in defiance of, every law that has been expounded in these pages, it nevertheless remains that none of these have been good pianofortes. Of the making of thump-boxes there is no end. Unfortunately for the public, musical ignorance is well-nigh universal, and the impostor finds it easy to palm off shoddy in place of the real article. Of course, it is quite true that bad pianofortes are soon found out, but when the inevitable discovery comes, the mischief has been done and the purchaser is, as usual, the victim. A student of the construction of good instruments cannot fail to be astonished that anyone should wish to turn out anything but the best. For, as one continues to investigate the multifarious problems that are continually suggested, the desire to overcome them and to produce perfect instruments becomes almost irresistible. Perhaps this is why the clever designer, if left to himself, often develops into a crank. And, indeed, there is not an industry on the face of the globe that has produced more cranks.

The files of the patent office are full of the ideas of unrewarded genius that has spent its time, its money and its enthusiasm in the unenviable task of producing innovations in pianofortes. No feature of construction has been left unimproved; yet how many of these inventions ever see the light? Few, indeed; and the fact is a sad commentary on the unpractical nature of genius in general.

These reflections lead one to the feeling that a fitting conclusion to a treatise on pianoforte construction may be made by giving particulars of some of the most famous and revolutionary inventions that at one time and another have been launched upon the unfeeling world of piano-making. Not all of these by any means can be denominated freaks; indeed there are the germs of most valuable developments in many of them. We shall consider a few of the really valuable ideas at least.

Among these primacy must be given to the screw-stringing device of Mason & Hamlin. This invention was intended to substitute a positive mechanical fastening for the tuning-pin, in place of the wooden wrest-plank. It consisted of a screw, threaded vertically in a socket, which was cut in a projecting shoulder on the iron-plate. As it extended below its socket, it was provided with an universal joint which ended in a hook. On this hook the string was wound, and was then free to pass on to the agraffe. A small T-hammer sufficed to turn the screw and the string was tightened or slackened as the screw turned in the threaded socket. The action was slow but sure, and the strings had the curious property of sharping under a test blow instead of the opposite, as is usual. The method of tuning was the same except that the screw turned in the opposite direction to the ordinary style and required much more turning to bring the string to the desired point. On the other hand, however, setting the pin was unnecessary, and the evils engendered by bad wrest-planks and sticking or twisting pins were unknown. Moreover, the turning of the screw involved very slight effort.

With all these advantages, however, the reverse motion and the slowness of action were fatal; and after several years of effort Mason & Hamlin gave up the attempt to popularize their invention, and let it drop. It is, indeed, unfortunate that this device did not become more popular, as in that case its many inherent advantages would doubtless have been emphasized and the bad points in it eliminated. Prejudice and the tuners, however, were against it, and it died.

The well-known house of Brinsmead in London has also experimented with a similar device, but it is not known with what success. One of the advantages held out by the makers of such string devices was the supposed facilitation of the work of tuning—that is to say, it was alleged that every musician could become his own tuner as soon as he had learned the theoretical principles of the Equal Temperament. The hope was delusive, however. Perhaps the professional tuners attended to this point.

Another similar but more successful device is being manufactured by the Wegman Piano Co. This is in the form of a fastening for the pin in the iron plate. The appearance of the plate and pin is not different from the usual design, but the tapered end is done away with and the pin, instead of being driven into the wooden wrest-plank, is fastened in the plate by means of the friction set up between the peculiarly bored hole and the back of the pin. A special twist is needed to fasten the pin when a string is drawn up to pitch, but otherwise the method of operation is not unusual. The device appears to be of value.

The sound-board has ever afforded a fertile field for inventive genius. It has been altered in every conceivable manner, but the old style continues to flourish with all its pristine activity. This is not to say that it is ideal and insusceptible of improvement. On the contrary, one cannot deny that many praiseworthy ideas have been patented for the purpose of improving it. The ribbing has been the subject of much attention from inventors. It is true that this method of giving strength and tension to the board is by no means perfect. Yet we find that the various devices proposed for the abolition of ribbing have almost uniformly failed. A large number of these failures owe their conditions to the lack of acoustical knowledge of the inventors. It has often been supposed that the enormous relative resonance power of the violin belly was connected in some way with the duplicate nature of the resonance table and the consequent hollow shape of the resonating body. This has been conclusively disproved, however, for it has been shown that the violin's special shape is given to it merely for the purpose of bearing the strain of its strings. Moreover, the tone and resonance of a violin have been reproduced by means of a vibrating diaphragm and a horn. This device, known after its inventor as the Stroh violin, satisfactorily disproves many cherished theories in regard to violin resonance. In spite of these facts we find that several patents have been taken out for pianoforte sound-boards, of which the guiding principles have been ingenious applications of the violin idea. The *"equilibré"* pianoforte of Frederic Mathushek was an example of this type. It seems passing strange that experimenters have not all become aware long ago of the essential differences between the resonance apparatus required for struck and for bowed strings.

There have been other and saner variations of sound-board construction. It has been suggested that the use of a double board composed of two cross-grained thicknesses glued to each other would obviate the necessity of ribbing and increase the power of resonance. There seems to be little doubt that there is the germ of a valuable idea in this, and if the notion is properly worked out, it will very likely produce valuable additions to our knowledge of the phenomena of resonance.

Unusual ideas have been less frequent in the domain of action-making. There have been several praiseworthy attempts to get rid of the troublesome, but hitherto necessary, tape in the upright action. The patent of Leo Battalia is one of these. He abolishes the tape and bridle wire, and substitutes a two-branched spring fork projecting from the jack. One branch works in a slot cut in the hammer butt and the other bears against the back check. The back stop is done away with and excellent repetition is assured, superior to that which is obtained by ordinary methods.

In the domain of pure scale design, we note the ever present and perennial notion of sympathetic strings. This idea has taken various forms. The most conventional development is, of course, the "duplex scale" of Steinway and others. This utilizes the waste ends of the strings and scales off lengths of them that correspond to aliquot parts of the vibrating length of each string, thus obtaining the advantage of sympathetic partial tones. Most of the ideas in this direction have gone further than this, however. Some makers have gone so far as to have a fourth string tuned to the octave of every three-string group. But this is surely unnecessary when we consider that the octave is, on the pianoforte, the strongest partial tone of any musical sound, and least of all needs adventitious aid.

There are many other similar devices used and unused that we should waste our time in considering. In any case the true test of the utility of an invention is use, and each one of these unusual notions that have been put on the market would have been universal long ago had they been uniformly practical and valuable.

We cannot close this hasty survey without mention of the remarkable innovation in action mechanism devised by Mr. Morris Steinert. Here the forcible hammer-blow is superseded by a gradual push on the hammer at the strings, executed through the interposition of an articulated double lever between the hammer and the jack. The result is to produce a different form of hammer attack and a noticeable modification in the coloring of the tone produced from the string. While the claims of the inventor are somewhat exaggerated, there is no doubt that Mr. Steinert has hit upon a valuable variation in the method of actuating the hammer, and his invention opens up new prospects of pleasure to the pianist.

If all these and the innumerable others have no other value, they at least teach that inventive genius and the hunger for improvement do not entirely sleep; that the pianoforte is continually being improved, and that many are spending their time in finding new ways of improvement. It shows that the value of the pianoforte to the community is sufficiently great to cause the expenditure of much valuable thought upon its mechanical and musical betterment. The fact that these things happen should console anyone who has ever thought that the limit of mechanical excellence had been reached.

The designing of a pianoforte is art with a big A. It demands of its practitioners the temperament of an artist and the skill of an excellent mechanic. There is no greater pleasure and no nobler work than the construction of an instrument equipped to give forth lovely tone and to interpret the inspired works of the masters of music. May the advancing years bring the pianoforte as much more of mechanical and musical excellence as the last two centuries have so richly imparted.

And now our task is done. It has been a labor of love to place the results of long study and much practical experience before those to whom this exposition of the principles of pianoforte construction might be expected to appeal. It has been far from easy to put into really intelligible and concise

English an explanation of certain of these laws; and if the reader finds here aught of vagueness or obscurity, may he blame the subject rather than the author. The latter has, as best he might, laid down the principles that underly the right building of the noblest musical instrument that man has yet devised. And in the contemplation of these principles he may properly be content to leave his patient readers.

APPENDIX A.
THE DEVELOPMENT OF THE PLAYER-PIANO.

Events are moving quickly in these latter days, and the conservative pianoforte trade is feeling the effect of the extraordinarily active spirit of constructive commercialism that is so pronounced a feature of the contemporary industrial movement. When the first chapters of the present work were in course of preparation, some two years ago, the pianoforte equipped with an interior playing mechanism was just beginning to be heard of; to-day its manufacture and marketing are recognized features in the policy of nearly all pianoforte houses. It would therefore be unwise to conclude the present treatise without certain observations on the player-piano question, although a truly philosophic temper would probably prefer that some further time elapse before any feature of the player-piano problem be considered in a work of the same scope and character as this. Abandoning the strict scientific view of our duty in this matter, however, we may better adopt a more popular *point d'appui* and round off this work with a few observations on the more important and essential underlying problems connected with this new and remarkable movement in the pianoforte world.

Had the exterior type of pianoforte playing device—the so-called cabinet-player, in fact—remained alone and supreme in the territory that it first opened to exploration and development, this work would contain no notice of any mechanism of the kind. But since the movement has spread until it comprehends the pianoforte itself, since, in the nature of things, such a development must profoundly affect the solution of the problems that confront the pianoforte maker in the construction of his instrument, it seems to be not only natural, but imperative, that we should devote some space to certain notes on the player-piano problem and its relation to the application of such acoustical and mechanical principles as are germane to the theory of pianoforte construction.

We are under no obligation to delve into the history of these ingenious devices. The plan of this work requires nothing of the sort. We may say, however, that the first impetus towards the production of a piano playing mechanism came about through the success of the self-playing organ which began to appear about fifteen years ago. Meanwhile various inventors had experimented with electrical devices and had succeeded in producing a mechanism that could be placed within the case of the instrument without entailing any great distortion of form. Such devices, however, were, with some exceptions, exceedingly mechanical in effect, and did little to show the possibility of adequately rendering pianoforte music through artificial means.

It was, however, through the successful development of mechanism for the automatic operation of organs that the true principles for piano-player construction began to come to light. Two leading manufacturers had both produced reed organs of a very superior kind, equipped with mechanical playing devices. The principle was pneumatic, and was applied through the medium of compressed air. The organs themselves were also operated on this principle, this being a return to the old force bellows system, adopted in the European harmonium, and always used in connection with the pipe organ. When developed to their highest point, these pneumatic self-playing organs produced superior musical effects, so that they became, and still are, well known and popular. The latest styles, indeed, rival the orchestra in their versatility and coloring, especially when operated by a skillful musician.

The pneumatic principle thus applied, and the success of the attempts to adapt it to the organ, led experimenters to emulate, and if possible improve upon, the early attempts at the practical manufacture of pianoforte-playing mechanism. Without going too much into details, it may be recorded that the two concerns previously referred to were nearly ready in 1896 to come out with such an instrument, and patents were granted in 1897 for a complete piano-player of the cabinet style, attachable to any piano, and easily detachable therefrom. Other patents soon followed, and other manufacturers fell into line, with the result that the great piano-player movement had soon begun in earnest. The productions of the different firms, of course, varied in details, but only two widely separated schools have developed, and inasmuch as both of these employ the pneumatic principle, which has triumphed over all others, and is now adapted unanimously by manufacturers who desire to render possible an approximation to artistic rendition of pianoforte music, it will be unnecessary to treat of any instruments constructed on other lines.

In the meantime it will be well to note that the above short sketch of the preliminary skirmishing, as it were, is intended to be nothing more than an outline, as the policy adopted throughout this entire work has been to avoid the historical view-point, as much as possible, and to confine ourselves strictly to the business in hand; namely, constructional principles and their application.

The pneumatic principle has been adopted in all the piano-players that we have occasion to survey, and its application has been in all cases essentially similar. Indeed, the two schools of construction differ, not in the application of the pneumatic principle, but in certain details of construction, which are important but not vital. One general description will be quite sufficient to acquaint the reader with the make-up of these instruments, and it will be easy to undertake any further explanations of important variations.

The underlying idea, upon which the whole player is built, may be described as arising from the knowledge that a bag or bellows of suitable material will collapse whenever the air is exhausted from it, and become inflated again when the air is permitted to rush into it, which happens as soon as the vacuum is destroyed. Now it is obvious that here, in these two processes, we have the possibility of producing a reciprocating motion, and the value of this is evident when it is remembered that the process of pianoforte playing, when reduced to its lowest terms, is essentially the combination of the alternate manual motions required to depress and release a key. Consequently, the matter of designing a pianoforte-playing machine is reduced to the problem of placing a bellows over a key, or in mechanical connection with it, in such a way that the inflation and deflation of the bellows will operate levers to depress and release the key. Thus far, it may be understood, we are dealing with elementary mechanical principles. But the questions arising from consideration of the control of these bellows are far more delicate, and require for their solution a high degree of mechanical talent. Let us see how the problem has been worked out.

A musical composition which is to be performed on the pianoforte by means of one of these "players," as they are called colloquially, is first reduced to a series of perforations on a long sheet, the perforations being of uniform width, but varying in length according to the duration of the musical tone for which each stands. The sheet is then wound upon a spool and is connected with motor mechanism which is adapted to draw it across a "tracker-board" pierced with holes, each of which corresponds to some hole in the sheet. The latter, when so drawn across the plane of the "tracker-board," is wound up on another spool, and the motor mechanism of the player is so arranged that the sheet can be re-wound on to its own spool when the whole composition has been played, so that it may be withdrawn from the "player," and another substituted in its place. The actual process of operation is as follows: The "player" is provided with foot pedals, which operate exhaust bellows, and thus maintain a reservoir bellows in a state of exhaust, on the same principle as in the reed organ. As long as the exhaust bellows are operated, and the reservoir is kept in a state of vacuum, it is possible to maintain an "exhaust chamber" within the "player" also in a state of vacuum. This exhaust chamber communicates with a "diaphragm chamber," in connection with the "tracker-board" hole, and with an "inflation and deflation channel" in connection with the striking pneumatic or bellows which depresses the pianoforte key. The connection with the "diaphragm chamber" is by means of a very small hole pierced in a leather diaphragm which is stretched between the "exhaust chamber" and the "diaphragm chamber," so that the latter will be in a state of partial vacuum. Resting on the leather diaphragm is a button, attached to an upright spindle which stretches through an orifice into the inflation and deflation chamber, and there operates a poppett valve which, in one position of the spindle, will close the chamber against the exhaust chest, while opening itself and therefore also the pneumatic to the outer air, and in another position will reverse the process, opening the chamber to the power of the vacuum in the exhaust and simultaneously closing itself and therefore the pneumatic to the vacuum, which will cause the latter to collapse, and thus bring down the key. Now, when a hole in the perforated sheet comes opposite a hole in the "tracker-board," an atmospheric communication is opened with the "diaphragm chamber," and air will immediately rush down into the "diaphragm chamber" and at once destroy the partial vacuum which existed there. As a consequence of this, the leather diaphragm will immediately rise to its fullest extent, influenced by the vacuum in the chamber above it, and will therefore push up the poppett valve. This action will open communication between the exhaust and inflation and deflation chambers and will expose the latter to the vacuum, while shutting off the outer air which has kept the pneumatic inflated. Thus the pneumatic will collapse, and the piano key will be held down until the closing of the "tracker-board" hole once more restores the partial vacuum in the "diaphragm chamber," thus permitting the poppett valve to sink, and reopening the connection between the pneumatic and the outer air, which re-inflates it and releases the key.

As will have been anticipated, there are endless small variations of detail in the construction of different "players," but they all work on the same principle, and the above description will be sufficient to give an idea of what goes on inside the "player" when the perforated sheet is put into position and drawn over the "tracker-board." Variations on the mechanical carrying out of these principles are dependent upon the ideas of the different makers. It can easily be understood that there is plenty of room for endless changes in details, and that every maker of "players" has his own special notions on the subject.

We have spoken above of the motor mechanism designed to move the perforated sheet across the "tracker-board," and to rewind it when required. It is clear that such a motor device must be very sensitive to changes in speed control, very light and very easily operated. In the search for the ideal device manufacturers have gradually separated themselves into two schools of practice, each being champions of one particular type of motor. These two schools of opinion and practice have adopted respectively the pneumatic and the clock-work motors. Both have virtues; neither are free from vices. It is no part of our plan to enter into didactic discussion of the relative merits and demerits of the two styles, but we shall confine ourselves to an exposition of the method whereby each is adapted to its required work, and shall point out the more obvious of the good and bad features of both.

The pneumatic motor has the initial advantage of simplicity and lightness. It consists of a number of bellows, usually three or five, which are arranged in series on a board and connected by passages with the exhaust chest. They are adapted to be collapsed and inflated alternately by means of the exhaust from the bellows of the "player," and are governed by valves so arranged as to cause one bellows to be open to the atmospheric air, and therefore inflated, while the next to it is simultaneously closed to the atmospheric air and exposed to the vacuum from the wind-chest, and therefore collapsed. This alternate process produces a motion which can, of course, easily be transferred by means of connecting rods to a crank-shaft, which by reciprocation produces a rotary motion, and also permits the take-up spool of the "player" to be connected with it by suitable gearing. The controlling valves are generally connected with the crank-shaft somewhat after the manner of the valves of a steam cylinder, and are operated by the motion of the shaft through suitable connecting rods. The reverse motion of the spool, for rewinding, is accomplished by gearing between the motor and spool, and the reversing lever, while operating this gear, also closes the valve between the exhaust reservoir bellows and exhaust chamber so as to permit the full power of the exhaust to be exercised on the motor when the rewinding is required. The speed control of the pneumatic motor is governed by another finger lever adapted to operate a valve which can entirely close the passage between the exhaust chest and motor board, the gradual opening or closing of which increases or diminishes the power of the exhaust upon the motor bellows and hence the rapidity with which they collapse and reinflate. This speed control combines simplicity and effectiveness.

In considering the less agreeable qualities of the pneumatic motor we have to note that a great deal of the alleged deficiency of the type arises from the fact that its operation depends upon the same agency as is employed for the striking pneumatics; namely, the exhaustion of air from the exhaust bellows reservoir. This means, of course, that the striking pneumatics and the motor are artificially brought into relations which would never naturally subsist between them. In consequence, there is a continual tendency on the part of one of the elements to monopolize the power reserve, to the detriment of the other. Thus, a fortissimo passage will tend to use up so much power that the motor will be slowed down; while, contrariwise, the latter, when driven at its highest speed, will take too much power from the pneumatics and prevent the expression of their highest dynamic forces. Here we touch upon the most serious defect of the pneumatic motor, and while we find the practical workings of these devices quite excellent, there is no doubt that they would be far more responsive and far lighter in operation if these fundamental defects did not exist.

The clock-work motor, on the other hand, is entirely separated from the striking mechanism, except as far as it is sometimes connected with the pedals for the purpose of winding the spring. Even this, however, is not a real interference with the striking pneumatics. The chief advantages of the clock-work motor are that it is built of steel and brass, instead of wood and leather; that it is independent of the rest of the player, and therefore always self-contained and free from extraneous influences; that rewinding is effected by the reserve power of the spring, and that the use of the pedals as in the pneumatic motor, is therefore not necessary.

Its disadvantages, as alleged by its critics, may be considered as follows: That it requires oiling and cleaning frequently, and that if neglected will rapidly become impaired; that it is sometimes slow in acceleration and retarding; that it is heavy and complicated, and that the winding, when done by pedals, is wasteful, and when effected by a handle, is tiresome.

The above tables of vices inherent in both types are by no means as terrible as they look, however, and experience seems to show that many of them do not appear in practical work. On the whole, the clock-work motor seems to have much in its favor, although the question still remains open, and time alone can show which is practically better.

It is neither necessary nor profitable to go into any considerable detail as to the pianoforte pedal operating devices, the soft stops, or other details of the sort. We may better employ the space at our command in a short discussion of the movement which has resulted in incorporating the mechanism described above into the case of the pianoforte itself. This movement is, of course, a natural outcome of the successful introduction of the exterior "player." The public soon began to find fault with the latter on account of the space it occupied, and also because of the annoyance incidental to its removal from the instrument for manual playing. It was not long before the makers of "players" were experimenting, with a view to using the waste space in the upright pianoforte for the purpose of including the "player" therein. The advantages of such a plan are obvious, provided that the actual mechanical difficulties can be overcome. These difficulties proved very stubborn at first, and it is not to be supposed that all are entirely overcome, even now.

It has been very hard, indeed, to arrange the mechanism in such a manner as to make all parts accessible for adjustment and repair. The results of any neglect of this important requisite are very serious. Makers should bend their first energies to the removal of all difficulties incidental to the obtaining of access to the playing mechanism or to the rest of the pianoforte, before they consider anything else. For example, it should be possible to remove the action or keys of the pianoforte without having to detach pipes and tubes.

Nor should it be difficult to disconnect the pumping apparatus, or some individual valve or pneumatic which may need attention.

Again, the manner in which the pneumatics strike the keys or action is very important. The earlier player-pianos generally had the pneumatics placed below the key-bed, so that they operated from the rear end of the latter, striking them upwards. This had the double disadvantage of inflicting a hard, rigid kind of blow, and of making the pneumatics very inaccessible. A better plan has lately been devised, which puts the pneumatics over the keys, so that they operate at the front ends, just back of the ivories. Some such method as this is excellent always, since it permits a considerable concentration of the mechanism and a consequent curtailment of the inconveniently long tubes leading from the "tracker-board" to the valve chambers. All these matters, however, are in process of practical development, and the future holds the key to the ultimate solution of any such problems.

In considering the influence of the "player" mechanism upon the pianoforte itself, we may note that the general adoption of these devices, if it occurs, will inevitably produce certain modifications in the action mechanism, as well as in the general design. There is no doubt that the ordinary action mechanism of the pianoforte will not prove strong enough to endure the furious onslaught of the "player," and it is questionable whether pianofortes constructed on the old plan will not more rapidly deteriorate when exposed to this wear and tear. The precise direction in which this modification is likely to come may not now be accurately determined, but it is probable that a general strengthening of centres and flanges will be the first result.

As for the distortion of the pianoforte case, this, as far as it now exists, may very easily be corrected. But it will not be easy to arrange the playing mechanism so as to avoid interference with the acoustical or mechanical forces of the pianoforte. For one thing, there is a great deal of machinery to put into a very small space, and for another there are certain parts of the pianoforte that must under no circumstances be touched. Thus the sound-board, the strings and the iron plate must be left severely alone. But the elimination of the Boston or double-rolling fall-board, and its replacement by something that will take less room, will provide a sufficient space to house the pneumatics and exhaust chamber above the keys. This is where they ought to be, and the only possible place where they can be reached without trouble or damage. The pumping apparatus must be kept away from the sound-board, and placed where it will do no harm; under the key-bed, necessarily, but not so as to interfere with the piano pedals or the resonance apparatus. Some portion of the bottom frame can usually be eliminated with advantage, and this will assist in providing the necessary space.

The position of the motor should be such that the minimum of waste occurs between the crank-shaft and the take-up spool. Thus, if possible, the motor ought to be above the key-bed. If it be of the clock-work type, it can hardly be placed anywhere else. Lastly, the whole of the exterior apparatus, such as levers, pedals, spool, etc., should be arranged to fold away or be covered up out of sight when the instrument is in use for manual playing.

While it has only been possible in this appendix to give the barest outline of the player-piano problem, the reader is besought to recollect that the industry is still new, and that the "present state of the art" hardly admits of any didactic assertions on principles of construction. We do not even know, today, whether the pneumatic principle will continue to prevail, or whether some new refinement of electric mechanism will not eventually surpass every device now known, both in responsiveness and convenience.

APPENDIX B.
THE SMALL GRAND.

It is a curious fact, but none the less characteristic of that most curious of industries—the pianoforte craft—that in it the development hypothesis, so familiar to all other branches of human endeavor here, appears not to be fully applicable. While the aim of the present treatise has been to systematize and codify, as it were, the laws that underly all right constructional methods, we have been forced to recognize that there is no appearance of any accurate and uniform generalization which may be applicable to the future guidance of pianoforte builders in their efforts to attain to the greatest perfection in later types. Although we have succeeded in laying down the broad and universal principles that govern intelligent practice of the art, yet we cannot fail to note that a progressive evolution is not yet possible. That is to say, there is no progressive synthesis in the art which shall carry us continually further from the original types, so that the ancient models shall become in time quite unrecognizable in the light of modern improvement. Rather would it seem that the course of improvement is leading us back to reversions towards the original types, and of this tendency the rise of the small grand pianoforte is one of the most striking illustrations.

It is not to be supposed that this reversionary movement is to be taken as implying a dissatisfaction with the methods that have grown up in the course of the last hundred years, and the systematization of which has been our task in the present work; it is rather that the tendency today is in the direction of utilizing the most modern methods in the resuscitation and further development of the type of pianoforte that was earliest in the field.

In other words, as the reader well knows, the last few years have seen a general tendency towards a revival of the grand, in forms suitable for modern ways of life, and with the advantages carried by the wealth of experience and practice on which the modern pianomaker can make unlimited drafts. This resuscitation has not taken the form of any attempt to bring the large-sized concert instrument into more popular use, but it has rather been a matter of evolving a new type out of the old, and of developing this latter along comparatively original lines. With the commercial success of such an experiment we are not here immediately concerned, but we have great and lively interest in the question of its constructional value and in the possibilities that are implied in its future development.

Without entering into wearisome detail, it may be stated that the last five years have seen a most systematic attempt on the part of leading manufacturers to construct and popularize a very small style of grand pianoforte, and to endow this new instrument, as far as possible, with the musical advantages possessed by the larger and older horizontal forms. The dimensions of the "small grand," as it has come to be known, range from a length of five feet to one of six, with width in proportion, and the smallest sizes are continually attracting greater attention on the part of experts. The idea is to reduce the dimensions to the very lowest point compatible with something approaching to grand pianoforte tone, and to make the general outline as beautiful to the eye as possible. The latter of these desires is easier of consummation than the former, and it has therefore appeared that some of the makers of these instruments have been somewhat apt to overlook truly musical results in deference to a public sentiment in favor of something that is graceful, if nothing else. In fact, when considering the small grand we are obliged to note that it has been developed, and is now being produced rather to appeal to that portion of the pianoforte-buying public that demands something for its homes more beautiful than the upright and less bulky than the large parlor or concert grand than in answer to any general cry for the better musical development of the instrument itself.

If we bear this fact in mind, and its truth is obvious to the student of pianoforte history, we can the more easily understand and appreciate the essential features of this latest development.

The small grand has been produced, we repeat, to please the public, and the public at large is not exclusively composed of musicians.

But even while acknowledging the probability of this statement, we need not conceal from ourselves that the small grand can thus fulfill a very useful function. Reduced to its lowest terms, it remains a grand pianoforte, with the action and touch so essentially associated with the horizontal form, and so immeasurably superior to anything that is found in even the best uprights. And here the small grand has an enormous advantage, nor does it appear that its truly musical and tonal development need be permanently stationary, if only the limitations of the instrument be appreciated, and work on it be directed with especial reference to its own size, and without dependence upon the traditions that have supported the building of larger forms.

In a word, the builders of small grands have the opportunity, if they care to avail themselves of it, to produce a form of miniature horizontal pianoforte that shall possess all the advantages of the large concert instruments, with the exception of the great tonal volume peculiar to the latter, and none of the disadvantages of bulkiness and ungracefulness. They can never hope to obtain the same tonal results from a 5-foot as from a 9-foot instrument; but they have the opportunity to popularize a touch and technique that is impossible of achievement for players of the upright, and a quality of tone that is equally unattainable on vertical instruments. Under all circumstances, it must be borne in mind that the results of small grand building, even when most carefully and skilfully executed, are essentially different from anything that has yet been produced in the tonal development of the pianoforte, and that no attempt to imitate the tonal properties of the large grand can be successful. The action and the touch are fit subjects for this kind of imitation, but such tonal quality as is susceptible of development is entirely original and indigenous to the miniature grand. The only legitimate field of inquiry along these lines, then, is that which has reference to the development and constructional principles of the small grand considered as a distinct type, and needing particular and definitely differentiated principles and methods.

Assuming the correctness of these premises (and their truth would appear to be obvious), we have to ask ourselves what is the exact nature of the problem which is set for solution, and wherein it differs from any that we have had to consider as yet. Bearing in mind that we are dealing with what is known as the "small grand," although it is marketed under various other names selected by different manufacturers, we can state the constructional problem in fairly definite and exact terms.

It is required to build a pianoforte in horizontal form, of which the extreme length shall preferably not exceed five feet and six inches, and which shall be compensated for shortening by means of extra widening; which shall have the lines of a larger grand, refined to the highest degree, and within which the greatest possible tonal value shall be contained.

Viewed thus, it appears that the principal factors to be considered are string-length and sound-board area. It is obvious that the diminution of the former and restriction of the latter are inevitable; and the net result must be seen in a radical alteration, if not deterioration, of the tonal property of the instrument. It remains to be seen how we shall set about to transform this disadvantageous condition into one that shall work for us, and in accordance with our desires. In other words, as we cannot get a sound-board containing, say "n" square feet of superficial area into a case that only contains $\frac{3}{4}$ "n" square feet of space, we must resign ourselves to the inevitable, and search for ways and means whereby the difficulty of putting into a quart bottle more than it will hold may be evaded, if not explained away.

And first, then, let it be remembered that the only line where-from we can safely base any calculation is that which leads in the direction of a continual refinement of the means of applying sound-board construction to the instrument. We must utilize every inch of the superficies; we must discover and apply methods for opening up the vibratory area to the impressions received from the strings in a manner superior to that which has been deemed sufficient when space has been at a discount. We must arrange bridges and bearing-bars so that the string-lengths may be stretched to the utmost, and, lastly, we must use such minute care in the treatment of the hammer-striking line that the inevitable "breaks" in the tone shall be minimized.

The intelligent reader will not fail to observe that we have put forth here a tolerably difficult set of requirements. But he will likewise be equally quick to note that ultimate success in small grand designing depends entirely upon the manner in which these conditions are met. If they are slighted or slurred, if the designer attempts to ignore them, he will find that failure will surely follow. On the other hand, it would be too much to say that even the most faithful and conscientious effort applied to the elucidation of the problem will under all circumstances have the desired effect. The conditions are unusual; in some cases they do not admit of any direct and positive settlement. But in so far as these conditions can be met, in so far as they are susceptible of solution, the designing of the small grand can properly be made successful.

It must be recollected that the "striking-point" of the hammers is a vitally important element in the success of pianoforte building. It is the one factor that cannot be trifled with, and in treating which there must be rigid adherence to rule. Now it is well known that the correct striking distance has been ascertained (as shown in the body of this work) to be at a point between one-seventh and one-ninth of the speaking length of the string, the exact place for each string being calculated with reference to the actual speaking length. As worked out in the best practice, the shortest and highest pitched strings have their striking points at about one-tenth of the speaking lengths, while the longer and lower pitched elements further down the scale are made to conform more closely to rule. Now it is obvious that the application of this law to the very much shortened strings of a small grand will result in distinctly unsatisfactory quantity and quality of tone. But it will not do for us arbitrarily to change the actual striking point, for that would change the position of the hammer line, and experience has amply demonstrated that no such idea will work. Inasmuch, therefore, as we are estopped from interfering with the striking point, as far as concerns the actual hammer line, it becomes necessary to discover some means for obtaining a somewhat greater length of string in proportion to the dimensions of case. Careful measurement will show that the higher strings do not fall under the classification of "dangerous." It is only when we approach the point where the overstringing begins that the disadvantage of decreased case length becomes apparent. The treble string-lengths at or near this place will be too great, if carried out according to the well-known and practiced laws of scale designing; while, if they are unduly shortened, the tensions and thicknesses will require to be submitted to such radical alteration as to make most unpleasant changes in the tonal quality and volume.

But while an absolute solution is out of the question, there is no doubt that we are able to find a fairly satisfactory substitute. There are two courses open to us. We are not permitted to make any great change in the tension, but, within certain limits, we may weight the string, and we may even stretch out its length, if we be very careful and watch out for every inch. The first method must always be used with caution. It is susceptible, and very easily, too, of improper application, and when abused becomes an enemy rather than a friend. In fact, the weighting of treble strings with iron or copper wire should be undertaken with the greatest caution, and only indulged in when the designer is absolutely unable in any other manner to obtain a proper vibrating length. The last two or three strings above the overstrung portion of the pianoforte may usually be wrapped without troublesome complications, but under no circumstances should the highest of these have a frequency greater than 128. On the other side, where the bass strings begin, this condition does not apply, for it is possible by means of suspension belly bridges, to increase the actual speaking lengths several inches. These suspension or extension bridges, as they are called, may also be used, though with caution, for the lowest treble strings. We have never advocated the splitting up of bridges, but there are cases, such as these, where unusual methods are quite unavoidable.

In the several ways thus sketched out, the designer of small grands may do something to overcome the manifest difficulties of his task. He may likewise take heart of grace when he approaches the matter of sound-board area, for in treating the string-lengths there appears a partial solution of the latter problem. In speaking of the use of suspension bridges we omitted to note that the position of these may be modified so as to give greater length to the speaking portions of the strings, by increasing the obliquity of the angle of the overstringing. Of course, this would be obvious, but it is perhaps not quite so clear that such adaptation will result in an opening out of spaces on the sound-board that are usually left severely alone. Moreover, if the necessary splitting up of the bridges be avoided by means of connecting strips of the same material, it is clear that the opening up of the sound-board may thus be carried up to the highest possible value.

Along such lines as these, it would seem, must the course of small grand designing be laid, at least as far as concerns the vital elements of string-length and sound-board area. There remains the question of the metal plate, and this deserves separate treatment.

We have taken pains already to insist upon the necessity for compromise in the building of small grands. Regarding the iron plate, we have to observe that great care must be taken to avoid undue massiveness, for this will entirely spoil the tone quality, as the other dimensions are not capable of supporting a large mass of metal without tonal deterioration. On the other hand, it is equally certain that we can afford to sacrifice nothing in the way of strength, as we purpose to have the highest tensions and the greatest lengths possible within the space limitations of our instrument. The ordinary form of plate, copied from the large grand, may very advantageously be modified by the adoption of a truss or arch construction, which will enable a large amount of metal to be cut away from the treble sides without sacrificing any strength.

Along such lines, as we have already said, the design of small grands must of necessity proceed. We feel that it would not be improper to repeat our formerly expressed opinion as to the nature and functions of the small grand. It has come into existence in answer to a public demand for something differentiated from the upright, possessing great beauty of outline, and yet adapted to the confined surroundings of contemporary domestic life. It is not and cannot be a rival of larger horizontal forms; it is physically estopped from the realization of such ambitions. But it has a place in the economy of the musical world, and such a place as nothing else would satisfactorily fill. Wielding the mighty influence of the name "grand pianoforte" and with the initial advantages over the upright that its form, touch and action imply, it would indeed be remarkable if the production of the small grand did not become more and more a part of the regular routine of all pianoforte manufacturing establishments. The design of its case will always, surely, be above criticism. It is out of our province to enlarge upon the details of case architecture, but it may be pointed out that such details as graceful trusses, well-designed lyre, and carefully molded curves do much to make or mar the future of a small grand, entirely apart from the excellence of its scale. The general effect should be that of lightness and grace; a touch of frivolity even will not be out of place. The little instrument is likely to find its way into homes where money is not always an object, and where the ability to enjoy the best that life contains is usually present. The designer will make no mistake if he keeps this in mind.

UNUSUAL METHODS OF CONSTRUCTION.

As the reader is well aware, the greater part of the present work has been devoted to an exposition of the broad principles underlying all right methods of pianoforte construction. We have devoted little space therefore to the elaboration of features without this classification, or to the consideration even of such ideas and methods as do not fall within the lines laid down in the theoretical portion of this treatise. Busily occupied, as we have been, with the development of acoustical and mechanical principles and their application along the most obvious and natural lines, we have been forced to neglect one of the most interesting studies that can be taken up by the investigator; to wit: the ideas, inventions and devices that have sprung from the brains of the numerous mechanical and acoustical geniuses who have illuminated the course of pianoforte history and development. Many of these ideas have proved impracticable under the stress of use; others, again, have been shown to be commercially unprofitable; a still larger number have flourished during a longer or shorter period or have been neglected by all others than their original inventors. The true place for a study of these neglected children of enthusiastic, if not always practical, brains is in a history of the pianoforte rather than in a technical treatise on construction.

[THE END.]

Booksophile
Your Local Online Bookstore

Buy Books Online from
www.Booksophile.com

Explore our collection of books written in various languages and uncommon topics from different parts of the world, including history, art and culture, poems, autobiography and bibliographies, cooking, action & adventure, world war, fiction, science, and law.

Add to your bookshelf or gift to another lover of books - first editions of some of the most celebrated books ever published. From classic literature to bestsellers, you will find many first editions that were presumed to be out-of-print.

Free shipping globally for orders worth US$ 100.00.

Use code "Shop_10" to avail additional 10% on first order.

Visit today
www.booksophile.com

Milton Keynes UK
Ingram Content Group UK Ltd.
UKHW010854211223
434780UK00005B/367